Home Office Research Study 194

Increasing confidence in community sentences: the results of two demonstration projects

by
Carol Hedderman,
Tom Ellis and
Darren Sugg

**A Research, Development and
Statistics Directorate Report**

London: Home Office

Home Office Research Studies

The Home Office Research Studies are reports on research undertaken by or on behalf of the Home Office. They cover the range of subjects for which the Home Secretary has responsibility. Titles in the series are listed at the back of this report (copies are available from the address on the back cover). Other publications produced by the Research, Development and Statistics Directorate include Research Findings, the Research Bulletin, Statistical Bulletins and Statistical Papers.

The Research, Development and Statistics Directorate

The Research, Development and Statistics Directorate is an integral part of the Home Office, serving the Ministers and the department itself, its services, Parliament and the public through research, development and statistics. Information and knowledge from these sources informs policy development and the management of programmes; their dissemination improves wider public understanding of matters of Home Office concern.

First published 1999

Application for reproduction should be made to the Information and Publications Group, Room 201, Home Office, 50 Queen Anne's Gate, London SW1H 9AT.

©Crown copyright 1999 ISBN 1 84082 252 X
ISSN 0072 6435

Foreword

In the 1995 Green Paper *Strengthening Punishment in the Community*, it was proposed that courts should be given greater discretion in their use of community sentences so that the amount and form of probation and community service would be tailored more closely to the individual offender.

The two demonstration projects described in this report were set up to test how far changes in approach, consistent with the principles set out in the Green Paper, might be achieved within the current law. The projects were successful in that they showed that more effective communication between the probation service and sentencers did lead to improved understanding. However, the projects also showed that simply encouraging sentencers, especially magistrates, to make more use of community sentences does not lead to significant changes in sentencing behaviour. The results suggest that such changes do require legislation.

Chris Lewis
Head of Offenders and Corrections Unit

Acknowledgements

A research exercise of this size can only be carried out with the good will and assistance of all those who come into contact with it. We would therefore like to thank all the probation service and court staff in Shropshire and Teesside who dealt so patiently and helpfully with our requests for information; Margaret Ayres, Jude Cotton, John Maggi, Peter Sheriff and Keith Ward, our colleagues in RDS, who provided local and national data on sentencing, policing and probation; and the judges, recorders and magistrates and probation staff in both areas for taking the time to be interviewed or to fill in questionnaires about the project. Our special thanks are due to: Gail Hunt, Elaine Lumley, Alistair Morrison, Roger Statham, Roger Ford and Paul Bushell for ensuring that we were kept up to date on changes in both areas and for smoothing our path in so many ways; Ed Mortimer for his work on the early stages of the data collection; Nick Holford and David Hughes for their assistance in collating court data; Nicola Hammond and Eulalia Pereira for their work on cleaning and analysing data; Chris May for his help with the analyses reported in Chapter 5 and Philip White for his advice on Chapter 3. The comments of Julie Vennard and other members of the National Steering Group on the penultimate draft were also invaluable. Finally, we would like to thank Alistair Morrison (ACPO Teesside) for ensuring that the data collection in Teesside went smoothly and for his unstinting efforts to obtain comparable data for Shropshire.

Contents

Summary

The Green Paper *Strengthening Punishment in the Community* (1995) proposed giving courts greater discretion in their use of community sentences so that the amount and form of probation and community service would be tailored more closely to the individual offender. Such a move was expected to enhance both sentencers and public confidence in community penalties. This was to be achieved by replacing probation, community service and combination orders by a single integrated sentence that would, depending on the offender and offence concerned, address one or more of three underlying objectives: restriction of liberty; reparation; and prevention of reoffending.

Responses from the Probation Service, magistrates and judges to the Green Paper showed general support for the idea of enhancing the content and image of community sentences, but not for legislation. For this reason, two demonstration projects were set up to test how far changes in approach, consistent with the principles set out in the Green Paper, might be achieved within the current law. One project was located in Shropshire, a comparatively affluent rural county, and the other in poorer and more urban Teesside.

Local steering groups determined exactly what changes to introduce, with the result that Teesside Probation Service used the project to push forward several initiatives, such as reviewing and revising the content of their probation programmes, whereas Shropshire decided that it should focus on ensuring that sentencers and the public had a much clearer idea of what actually happened to someone serving a community sentence.

Changes common to both areas included:

- providing sentencers with more detailed information about the content of community penalties;

- giving sentencers an opportunity to be more specific about what they would like pre-sentence reports to cover;

- inviting sentencers to comment on the range and content of community service (CS) provision and enabling them to tailor CS so that it involved caring for the disadvantaged or learning job-related skills; and

- enabling sentencers to seek feedback on completion rates.

The demonstration projects ran from 1 April 1997 to 31 March 1998 and were evaluated using a number of different techniques and data sources, including:

- interviewing and sending postal questionnaires to sentencers and probation staff;

- collecting sentencing information from court and probation records before and after the projects began;

- observing court proceedings and attending local steering group meetings; and

- obtaining copies of the documentation generated by the projects.

In considering the results of the projects, it is important to recognise that they were set up before the Home Affairs Committee's (1998) investigation into alternatives to custody began and that diversion from custody was never an explicit objective for either project.

Sentencers' views

The proportion of magistrates who saw probation with additional requirements as primarily concerned with the prevention of reoffending increased significantly during the demonstration period. There was a similar shift in Teesside magistrates' perception of straight probation. Both before and after the projects began, CS was seen as a way for the offender to put something back into the community (reparation), combination orders as preventing reoffending and prison primarily as a way of restricting an offender's liberty (incapacitation).

The demonstration projects appeared to affect magistrates' satisfaction with the information they received about the number of places on CS and probation programmes and when an offender would start a specified activity. About half of the magistrates surveyed in the 'before' period were satisfied with this, compared with nearly two-thirds in Shropshire and nearly three-quarters in Teesside.

Three-quarters of magistrates in both Shropshire and Teesside were 'very' or 'fairly' well informed about probation programmes before the demonstration projects began, but this rose to around 90 per cent in the 'after' period. The main change was in the number who described themselves as 'very' well informed. They also became better informed about the content of community service orders.

Magistrates in both areas felt more confident that they could tailor sentences to individual offenders as a consequence of the demonstration projects. This change was statistically significant. Many thought that there had been more changes to the range of probation programmes and types of CS available than had actually occurred. This reflects the fact that they were much better informed about what was available because of the efforts the two probation services had put into disseminating this information.

A minority of sentencers would like to be able to combine sentences in new ways. They were most interested in being able to combine a short period of custody with community penalties.

The majority of magistrates in both areas were 'always' or 'frequently' influenced in their choice of sentence by pre-sentence reports (PSRs) and most thought that PSR proposals were generally appropriate. A majority of magistrates said they would always request a PSR when considering a community disposal. This was true of only a minority of judges.

Crown Court sentencers tended to view using community penalties as 'taking a risk'. They were only prepared to do so if such a proposal came from a PSR writer whose opinion they respected. Sentencers were equivocal on whether more proposals for custody in PSRs would increase their confidence in the Probation Service in general.

Most magistrates welcomed the introduction of checklists, which caused PSR writers to focus on particular issues, and adjournment forms, which indicated sentencers' views on the seriousness of a case and the sorts of sentence they were leaning towards.

Sentencers in the 'after' period felt significantly better informed about supervision arrangements for all types of community order than in the 'before' period. In Shropshire, magistrates' satisfaction with the supervision and enforcement of all community penalties improved during the demonstration project. In Teesside the change was only significant in the case of probation orders with requirements and combination orders. Crown Court sentencers' satisfaction with enforcement declined. They were concerned partly about probation officers being too slow to take breach action, but their comments also concerned aspects of the process that were beyond the control of the Probation Service.

The apparently contradictory finding that the majority of sentencers wanted feedback in individual cases but that most never asked for it, may reflect the fact that they do not want this information on *every* individual they sentence, but on the few where they are especially concerned about offenders' progress. However, sentencers were keen to have aggregated data on the extent to which offenders complete programmes, and whether attendance leads to changes in attitudes and reconviction, in order to better judge the value of particular programmes and types of order.

Probation perspective

Nearly three-quarters of probation staff considered that restriction of liberty (incapacitation) was the main purpose of prison. No one thought its main objective was to rehabilitate. Four out of five probation officers surveyed thought that the main aim of a straight probation order or a probation order with additional requirements was to reduce reoffending; and the latter was the only sentence where rehabilitation was considered to be the main aim by more than 10 per cent of respondents. This runs counter to the idea that probation officers still see their primary function as 'to advise, assist and befriend offenders'.

Although most respondents said that the demonstration project had not affected the *frequency* with which they came into contact with sentencers, most said the *quality* of such contact had improved.

Most respondents thought a PSR was *essential* in all cases where a community sentence or custody was being considered – the exact proportion varied with the type of sentence. The remainder believed this was generally advisable but not essential, with the exception of one Teesside respondent who thought PSRs were rarely necessary.

One-third of the probation officers who took part in the postal survey were prepared to see PSRs explicitly propose custody. Some explained this by reference to the need to safeguard the public, but the most commonly given reason was that this would increase sentencer confidence in PSRs. The reasons given by those who felt that PSRs should never explicitly propose custody included the belief that custody had no positive effect and that it would simply be window-dressing (because sentencers already know custody is an option). Two of those interviewed thought that such a change might make sense at the Crown Court, rather than at the magistrates' court, because of the proportion of cases dealt with there that were serious enough to merit custody.

Over 40 per cent of those who responded to the postal survey thought that the targeting of PSR sentencing proposals had improved since the projects began, and a similar proportion thought that the clarity of PSRs had improved. About half the rest felt that the lack of change reflected the fact that PSR proposals and the clarity of PSRs required no improvement.

Among those who attended magistrates' courts, most viewed improvements in the quality of PSRs as being a consequence of changes brought about through the demonstration projects, particularly the use of checklists which showed those factors magistrates wanted the PSR writer to concentrate on in particular cases, and indications about the seriousness with which the bench viewed the case and even the sentence they were considering. Three of the eight probation staff interviewed in Teesside attributed the improvement there in PSR quality to a separate initiative that started prior to April 1997.

One of the ways in which the demonstration projects were expected to enhance the credibility of community sentences was by making sentencing pronouncements clearer, in that offenders were told why they were being sentenced in particular ways and what would happen should they fail to comply. However, over half (13) of those who attended court regularly in Shropshire said this rarely or never happened, as did slightly less than half (11) of those in Teesside. Our own smallscale observation in a magistrates' court in each area confirmed that sentencing pronouncements were rare.

The techniques used to promote compliance in either area seem to have been largely unaffected by the demonstration project. The most common suggestion for improving compliance was to make the requirements of an order clearer to an offender at the start of an order.

When offenders did fail to comply, respondents in both areas suggested that it would be helpful if breach proceedings were made faster and simpler. (In fact during the project, Shropshire reduced the time from issuing a summons for breach to the court hearing from six weeks to 14 days.) Respondents also suggested that supervisors should be more willing to breach offenders.

Probation interviewees were asked to comment on the fact that the sentencer survey showed they were keen to receive feedback on individuals and programmes, whereas the postal survey of probation staff showed they were rarely asked to provide it. Senior managers in both areas described a number of steps they had taken to try to provide such information more routinely (without being asked for it). For example, probation notice boards had been set up in Shropshire courts, and the Service had offered sentencers more opportunities to visit schemes when they would have a chance to discuss completion rates with probation staff. Most of those interviewed said they had tried as many different techniques as they could think of to provide sentencers with such information.

Of the probation staff who completed questionnaires, most commented very positively on the training they had received. They also thought the projects had given magistrates a better understanding of the community sentence options that were available locally. However, some of those interviewed, particularly in Teesside, were concerned that the training had not been focused sufficiently on such issues as suitability and risk.

Among the other positive effects respondents attributed to the community sentence demonstration projects were:

- increased use of probation programmes;

- improved relationships with sentencers; and

- better understanding of the issues sentencers wanted PSRs to concentrate on.

A sizeable minority (41%) however, thought, that despite the impact of the project there was still a lot of work to be done, particularly in improving probation/sentencer communication and sentencer training. A smaller number saw the projects as having negative effects:

- extra work;

- more PSRs, each one taking longer to prepare;

- *less* appropriate sentencing, with sentencers 'overusing' additional requirements.

Impact on sentencing

There was an increase in the proportion of offenders being fined and receiving community sentences at the Crown Court in Shropshire and a decrease in the proportion being imprisoned. The numbers involved were small, but the changes were statistically significant. There was no other evidence that the demonstration projects encouraged the greater use of community penalties as an alternative to custody. Indeed, the overall use of community penalties in magistrates' courts in Teesside actually declined during the demonstration project. The reasons for this are not obvious.

The only sentencing change common to both areas and both court levels was that the proportion of cases receiving a probation order with additional requirements rose, possibly reflecting greater faith in the power of this particular form of community penalty to prevent reoffending. To some extent the increase in magistrates' courts seems to have been brought about by magistrates using such sentences without adjourning for PSRs. When PSRs were available, the proportion of such sentences which matched proposals increased in Teesside and decreased in Shropshire.

At the Crown Court, the increased use of probation with requirements was associated with the sentencing of a broad range of offences; however, at the magistrates' court, sentencing behaviour changed most (although not exclusively) in relation to drunken drivers and those convicted of driving while disqualified. As the increased use of probation orders with requirements was generally associated with a fall in the use of community service, this may explain why some probation staff thought that sentencing had become less appropriate.

Media reporting

A separate but parallel study (Hansen, 1999) examined whether and how local media reporting of sentencing changed during the course of the demonstration projects. Samples of the main local newspapers were examined for 12 weeks before and 12 weeks after the demonstration projects began. This revealed that there were 3,616 articles on crime and/or sentencing in the 'before' period and 3829 in the 'after' period.

Most of these articles focused either on crimes committed or on the investigation and prosecution process. Only one-quarter mentioned sentencing. It is also noteworthy that sentencing almost never hit the front page (3% of 273 articles, compared with 10% of all crime reporting). They also tended to be shorter than articles on other aspects of crime.

Interestingly, while sex, violence and theft were discussed in half of all newspaper reports on crime, motoring was the next most common offence to be discussed; and its coverage increased from 7 per cent to 13 per cent in the 'after' period in Teesside. It is not possible to say whether this reporting led to the change in or was a product of sentencing.

Conclusions

The demonstration projects showed that relationships between the Probation Service and sentencers could be improved through better communication and working more closely together. Certainly most of those involved in the two projects viewed them as worthwhile because they had this effect. However, the extent to which such improvements affected sentencing practice was limited, particularly at the magistrates' courts.

The main sentencing change that did occur – an increase in the use of probation orders with requirements – was largely at the expense of other community sentences and related mainly to summary cases. This raises a number of questions about the targeting of such demanding (and expensive) sentences. It indicates that more work needs to be done to ensure that group work accessed through a statutory requirement to attend is not viewed as the only effective form of community sentence. To this end a new study into the rehabilitative potential of community service is already being planned, using Crime Reduction Programme funding.

The sentencing changes also highlight the need to ensure that decisions about effectiveness are tempered by concerns about proportionality. The lack of a clear tariff for community sentences makes this difficult to achieve.

Overall, the demonstration projects showed that better communication improved relations between the Probation Service and sentencers, and that this was something both sides welcomed. While this is undoubtedly an important first step in promoting the greater use of community sentences, the results of this study suggest that such improvements alone will not lead to a significant increase in the use of community penalties.

I Introduction

In 1995 the (then Conservative) government published a Green Paper *Strengthening Punishment in the Community* (Home Office, 1995b) which proposed giving courts greater discretion in their use of community sentences, so that the amount and form of probation and community service would be tailored more closely to the individual offender. Such a move was intended to make community sentences more effective and, by so doing, to enhance both sentencer and public confidence in them. This was to be achieved by replacing probation (with and without additional requirements), community service and combination orders with a single integrated sentence that would, depending on the offender and offence concerned, address one or more of three underlying objectives: restriction of liberty; reparation; and prevention of reoffending.

Comments received during the consultation period following the Green Paper's publication revealed general support for the further development of community sentences as a means of providing an element of punishment and deterrence as well as rehabilitation. A majority of the sentencers and probation staff who responded were also keen to see greater clarity about the purpose and content of community sentences and a wider range of options and information available to the courts. However, the proposal for a single integrated community sentence received a mixed reaction. Some respondents suggested that the current range of community options was sufficient. Others were concerned that a new sentence would require additional resources without there necessarily being any offsetting savings.

In order to test the potential demand for a new integrated sentence, the Home Office set up two hypothetical sentencing exercises in May and June 1995 using real, but anonymised, cases. The first involved 36 lay magistrates, the second five stipendiary magistrates and 13 judges and recorders. The results showed:

- lay and stipendiary magistrates used more custody and fewer community penalties than had occurred when the cases were actually sentenced; the opposite was true of judges and recorders;

- sentencers combined different elements far more often than in real life, with more than 70 per cent of sentences containing more than two elements;

- in nine out of ten cases additional requirements were made mandatory so that failure to comply could lead to breach and a return to court;

- some of the combinations used were not possible under existing legislation, but this was usually because of the length of the orders rather than their content;

- the elements most commonly used together (probation supervision and unpaid work) were already available in the form of a single sentence – the combination order;

- discussions with the sentencers who took part in the sentencing exercises also suggested that there was considerable support for better liaison between sentencers and probation services and for developing the range of supervision opportunities available locally (Mortimer and Mair, 1996).

Of course, this exercise was smallscale and artificial and no claims can be made about the likelihood of the findings being replicated in real life. However, it does suggest, first, that sentencers may not be making full use of the discretion they already have to tailor sentences to offenders, and, second, that if the findings were replicated in real life the increased use of mandatory additional requirements and longer orders could lead to a considerable increase in the cost of community sentences.

Taken together, the results of the sentencing exercise and the broader consultation process suggested that, rather than immediately legislating for a new integrated sentence, it would be preferable to set up demonstration projects to see how far changes in approach, consistent with the principles set out in the Green Paper, might be achieved within the current law.

The scope of the demonstration projects

The process of choosing two areas to host the community sentence demonstration projects (CSDP) began with the Association of Chief Officers of Probation (ACOP) issuing an invitation to all 54 probation areas in England and Wales to make initial expressions of interest. Twenty four areas responded, indicating that there was widespread support for the idea of demonstration projects. Several of the areas who did not volunteer explained that it was only because of the pressure of other commitments, such as taking part in HMI Probation area inspections, or moving over to the computer system for holding case records (the case records and management system, or CRAMS), being introduced nationally.

Areas were shortlisted according to the following criteria:

- that one area should contain a sizeable urban centre and the other should be rural;

- at least one magistrates' court and the main Crown Court centre in each area should be willing to participate;

- the Chief Probation Officer and other senior probation staff should be prepared to make significant changes to the way their service operated in terms of providing information to the courts and altering programme provision if this was required.

The final choice of areas was made by the Lord Chancellor's Department (LCD).

By the summer of 1996, it was agreed that Teesside and Shropshire Probation Services should host the demonstration projects, and a National Steering Group was convened with representatives from the Home Office and LCD, the Probation Inspectorate, the Association of Chief Probation Officers, the Magistrates' Association, the Judicial Studies Board, the Justices' Clerks Society, the Central Probation Council, the Probation Managers Association, the Law Society and the two project areas. Each project area also formed a Local Steering Group, chaired by the Resident Judge, with representatives from the local courts and Probation Services.

The National Steering Group was responsible for overseeing the project as a whole, providing advice and guidance to the project areas as required, devising materials for training and considering how lessons learned during the project should be disseminated.

The overall aim of the community sentence demonstration projects was to show whether changes in sentencing practice and better targeted community sentences could lead to more effective sentencing within existing resources and (thus) to an increase in sentencer and public confidence. Exactly how this was to be achieved was to be determined locally, although both Local Steering Groups were asked to begin by reviewing and, if necessary, improving a number of different aspects of existing practice:

- the information the probation service provided to the courts on the availability of constructive programmes of activity as part of supervision;

- the range of additional requirements which could be attached to probation supervision;

- indications from sentencers about what they would like pre-sentence reports (PSRs) to address in individual cases;

- the clarity of sentencing pronouncements so that the content and purpose of sentences were made clear and offenders knew what was expected of them;

- the use of probation staff in court;

- the enforcement of community sentences.

The only limits imposed on what changes the areas could make were that these should be consistent with existing legislation and that the projects should only target the sentencing of adult offenders. The latter decision was only reached after much deliberation, as the desire to improve the sentencing of young offenders was weighed against the difficulties of expanding the scope of the projects and involving additional (and non-criminal justice system) agencies in the projects. Eventually, the National Steering Group decided that youth court proceedings should not be included because they are closed to the public and a central aim of the demonstration projects was to make the reasons underlying the use of community penalties for particular cases more apparent to the public. It was difficult to see how the former might be maintained while trying to achieve the latter.

One final point about the way the projects were set up is worth noting; they were initiated before the Home Affairs Committee's (1998) investigation into alternatives to custody began and diversion from custody was not made an explicit objective.

The scope of the evaluation and methods used

The evaluation was designed to address ten main questions about the impact of the demonstration projects in each area:

- did the Probation Service improve the range of community service or probation programmes?

- did the Probation Service improve the information available to sentencers about community service or probation programmes?

- did sentencers seek and/or receive more feedback on success rates?

- did sentencers give probation officers clearer guidance when requesting PSRs?

- did sentencers express more confidence in community sentences?

- did sentencers make clearer sentencing pronouncements?

- did the use of community sentences increase during the demonstration period?

- was there an improvement in enforcement action?

- did the sentencers and probation staff involved in the projects think they had been a success and what other changes would they like to see?

- did newspaper, TV or radio reporting of local sentencing decisions and the use of community sentences alter?

In considering the answers to these questions it is worth noting that, officially, the demonstration projects ran from 1 April 1997 to 31 March 1998 – but these are, of course, artificial cut-off points. The projects built on some existing practice, and they have affected practice and will continue to affect it now that the projects are officially finished. Thus, it is possible that results reported reflect changes which had already begun before the demonstration projects were implemented; and some of the changes brought about by the projects may not have fed through into practice until the evaluation ended. It is also worth noting two further points. First, this report focuses on the *immediate* changes associated with the demonstration projects. In due course a study of two-year reconviction rates will investigate how any sentencing changes that occurred during the demonstration period affected reconviction. Second, it was recognised from the outset by the national and local steering groups and the research team that it would be inappropriate to compare the two project areas in the sense of seeing one as having achieved more or better things than the other. The project areas were chosen to reflect quite different conditions and, as Chapter 2 shows, that affected what they could achieve and also on what they chose to focus.

In designing the evaluation, two approaches were considered. The possibility of comparing Shropshire and Teesside with similar (control) areas was rejected on the grounds that it was unrealistic to expect to find two other areas which were similar enough on the relevant characteristics and because, even if such areas did exist, they were unlikely to remain unchanged during the course of the projects on the measures described above. We therefore decided to obtain as much information as possible about each Probation Service and the courts included in the study *before* each project began, and to collect the same information *after* the projects were implemented. We were concerned to investigate not only what had changed but also how the changes had come about (i.e. to carry out a *process* as well as an *outcome* evaluation). The full evaluation involved:

- examining centrally held statistics on each area;

- collecting and analysing data from court and probation records about a six-month *before* period (January to June 1996) and for six of the last seven months of the demonstration period (which ended in March 1998) – the *after* period[1];

- interviewing senior sentencers at the start and towards the end of the demonstration period;

- sending out postal questionnaires to all magistrates in both areas at the start and end of the project;

- informal discussions with senior probation staff at the start of the project and then formal interviews with them and other key probation staff towards the end of the project;

- sending postal questionnaires to all relevant probation staff at the end of the project (i.e. prison-based, family-court, welfare and youth-court staff were excluded);

- observation of a small sample of cases sentenced in Teesside and Shrewsbury magistrates' courts;

- researchers attending meetings of the Local and National Steering groups and receiving copies of any relevant documents throughout the course of the projects.

Initially, it was thought the projects should only cover the busiest magistrates' courts (Hartlepool and Teesside, Shrewsbury and Telford) in the areas, along with the Crown Court centres (Teesside and Shrewsbury). However, the Local Steering Committees quickly decided that the projects should cover all the courts in each area as this would ensure that maximum benefit was derived from the projects. This also simplified administrative arrangements such as setting up briefing and training events for sentencers.

It was not feasible to monitor directly the impact of the community sentence demonstration projects on public confidence, partly due to resource constraints but mainly because existing research shows that public opinion is largely uninformed by sentencing practice (e.g. Hough and Roberts, 1998).

---

1   Data were collected on a seven-month 'after' period to allow for the possibility that the Christmas and New Year holidays might have a distorting effect on the number of cases dealt with by the courts in each area. This proved to be the case, so the 'after' period examined is September to November 1997 and January to March 1998.

Instead, changes in media reporting of sentencing were used as a proxy measure of changes in public opinion. The contract for this work was awarded to Anders Hansen of Leicester University who is an expert in media analysis. This part of the evaluation considered changes in the overall levels of crime reporting in the local media in Teesside and Shropshire, changes in the extent and tone of reports about the use or supervision of community sentences, and the local and national impact of any publicity generated by the demonstration projects.

Structure of the report

Chapter 2 describes the characteristics of the two demonstration areas when the projects began, and describes some of the main changes introduced during the course of the projects. The next two chapters, respectively, examine the impact of the projects from the sentencer and probation perspectives. Chapter 5 considers how sentencing practice changed during the period covered by the projects; and in Chapter 6 key findings from the evaluation are reviewed and general conclusions drawn about the value of the demonstration projects.

2 The demonstration projects

In considering the impact of the community sentence demonstration projects it is important to know what the two project areas looked like at the time the demonstration projects commenced, what changes their Local Steering Groups (LSGs) planned, and which ones were actually implemented.

Social composition and criminal justice profile

Teesside is densely populated, with just under 560,000 people living within 597 square kilometres. About 2 per cent of the population are from an ethnic minority group. The area comprises four unitary authority areas (Middlesbrough, Stockton-on-Tees, Hartlepool and Redcar, and Cleveland), with two major conurbations of Middlesbrough and Stockton-on-Tees and several other large towns. At the start of the project the unemployment rate was 14 per cent, compared with just over 8 per cent nationally, and the area was designated a special priority area in securing reinvestment and urban renewal (ONS, 1997). As Table 2.1 shows, the reported crime rate in the Cleveland police force area (which covers Teesside) is higher than the national average and the clear-up rate is lower.

In contrast, Shropshire is sparsely populated and rural, with a population of 420,000 spread over 3,488 square kilometres. About 1.5 per cent of the population is from an ethnic minority. The two largest towns are the county town of Shrewsbury and Telford – a new town. The area as a whole is prosperous, with a lower-than-average rate of unemployment (around 7%), but there are pockets of rural and urban deprivation. Shropshire is policed by the West Mercia force. It has a lower recorded crime rate and lower clear-up rate than the rest of the police force area and than the national average (see Table 2.1).

Table 2.1: Crime profile by police force area 1996[2]

	National average	Cleveland	Shropshire	West Mercia
Recorded crime per 100,000 population	9,719	14,058	7,115	7,383
No of recorded offences	5,036,553	78,608	29,977	82,254
% cleared up	26	24	22	26
No of indictable offences cautioned and convicted	491,391	8,693	Not available	7,364
Convicted only	300,580	4,566	1,747	4,878

The courts

In 1996 (the year before the demonstration projects started) just over 1,700 defendants were tried at Teesside Crown Court, 85 per cent of whom were convicted. Around 7,500 defendants were proceeded against in the three Petty Sessional Divisions (PSDs) of Teesside, Hartlepool and Langbaurgh East, 49 per cent of whom were convicted and sentenced by magistrates and 17 per cent of whom were sent to the Crown Court for trial (Home Office, 1997a).

There were 376 lay magistrates serving in Teesside at the time the demonstration project began. The area is also served by several visiting stipendiary magistrates. After consulting local sentencers, it was agreed that the stipendiaries would not be asked formally to take part in the project because of the difficulties involved in arranging the one-off training sessions this would necessitate. Teesside Crown Court's Resident Judge is assisted by five permanent Judges and a range of High Court Judges, visiting Circuit Judges, recorders and assistant recorders. Any senior sentencers who regularly sat in Teesside were invited to participate in the project and their views were sought on its impact during the research.

In 1996 just under 500 defendants were tried at Shrewsbury Crown Court, 89 per cent of whom were convicted. Approximately 2,700 defendants were proceeded against in the PSDs of Bridgnorth, Drayton, Ludlow, Oswestry, Shrewsbury and Telford, of whom 47 per cent were tried and convicted by magistrates, with 19.5 per cent being sent to the Crown Court for trial (Home Office, 1997a).

---

2   National and force level figures are taken from *Criminal Statistics*, 1996 (Home Office, 1997a). Figures for Shropshire were specially generated by the Research, Development and Statistics Directorate of the Home Office.

At the start of the demonstration project in Shropshire all 269 lay magistrates, together with the permanent stipendiary magistrate, were invited to participate in the project and in the research. At Shrewsbury Crown Court the Resident Judge is occasionally assisted by visiting judges and recorders, but when court business becomes exceptionally busy cases are also sent to neighbouring Crown Court centres. For this reason only the Resident Judge participated directly in the demonstration project.

The Probation Services

The Teesside Probation Service is managed by the Chief Probation Officer and four Assistant Chief Probation Officers (ACPOs) and two Assistant Chief Officers (ACOs). The Service employs just over 200 staff[3] and runs one probation hostel and one bail hostel.

According to Probation Statistics, 921 probation orders and 581 community service (CS) orders commenced in Teesside in the year before the demonstration project began (Home Office, 1997b)[4]. At that time the Teesside Service was running seven programmes that were available across the whole probation area and could be used either as an additional requirement or, in a small number of cases, on licence. These are summarised in Table 2.2.

Table 2.2: Teesside's probation programmes at the time the demonstration project commenced

Name of programme	Length
Change your ways in 40 days (probation centre)	40 x 0.5 days
Victim awareness	4 x 0.5 days
Alcohol awareness	4 x 0.5 days
Drug awareness	4 x 0.5 days
Citizenship	4 x 0.5 days
Car offender	4 x 0.5 days
Handling conflict	4x 0.5 days or 8 x 0.5 days

The Shropshire probation service is managed by one Chief Officer, two ACPOs and one ACO and employs just under 50 staff. The Service does not run a hostel, but has service-level agreements with neighbouring areas which provide this facility.

---

3   Teesside and Shropshire staffing figures include whole-time equivalents.
4   The number of orders imposed by Teesside's courts and the number of orders commencing under probation supervision differ because some orders imposed by the courts will be supervised by other Probation Services and some orders commencing in Teesside will have been imposed by courts outside the area.

Two hundred and ninety-nine probation orders and 316 CS orders commenced in Shropshire in the year before the demonstration project began (Home Office, 1997b). At that time the Probation Service was running seven programmes, six of which were available across the county. The induction programme was only available in Oswestry, Shrewsbury and Telford. Very occasionally (for perhaps five or six offenders per year), the Service also made use of neighbouring areas' programmes. A drug-education programme was also being developed as the demonstration project began.

Table 2.3 summarises the programme provision in Shropshire at the time the demonstration project commenced.

Table 2.3: Shropshire probation programmes at the time the demonstration project commenced

Name of programme	Length
Induction, assessment and offending behaviour group	6 x 1.5 hours
Sex-offender programme	10 x 1 day per week
Alcohol-education programme	4 x 2.5 hours
Anger management	3 x 6 hours
Motoring-education programme	8 x 1.5 hours
DRIVE (car maintenance) project	Not specified
Employment options	8 x 6 hours

Shropshire also hosted the Specific Training for Offenders on Probation (STOP) project from October 1995 to December 1997, which examined the extent to which offenders under probation supervision had problems with basic skills and dyslexia and sought to design a model to support such offenders using mentors and special training.

Changes in Teesside

A Local Steering Group (LSG) was convened in Teesside immediately after the initial Home Office visit to the area (summer 1996), comprising the Chief Probation Officer, two ACPOs, the magistrates who chaired the three local benches, the Chair of the Probation Committee and the Clerks to the Teesside and Hartlepool Justices, and chaired by the Resident Judge. At the LSG's first substantive meeting in September 1996 a Home Office representative described the national aims of the demonstration projects. The subsequent discussion made it clear that both sentencers and the Probation Service in Teesside were keen to play a full and active part in this project, which they saw as being a partnership between the two groups and not simply about the Probation Service providing a better service to sentencers. The main source of concern was whether all the changes the group was keen to implement could be put in place by the time of the official launch in Teesside on 16 April 1997. Another concern was to ensure that all those working in the criminal justice system, such as court clerks and local defence solicitors, were aware of the project.

Over the subsequent few months the LSG gave consideration to:

- a review of existing probation programmes to ensure that magistrates knew what was available and were happy with the current provision;

- the need for new activities on CS;

- plans for training sentencers and probation staff;

- the content of new sentencing pronouncements that were intended to ensure that offenders fully understood why they had a particular sentence imposed on them;

- the availability of feedback to the courts on individual offenders and on the performance of probation programmes or CS placements.

The Probation Service reviewed and revised the range of programmes available as a statutory requirement that might be made part of a probation order. One change was to replace the Probation Centre programme 'Change Your Ways' with one called 'Thinking Straight on Probation' which was based on the most up-to-date empirical evidence on what works in changing offenders' attitudes and behaviour. The remaining programmes were all relaunched in January 1997 at an event attended by six Crown Court Judges, senior magistrates from the area, senior police officers, solicitors and Probation Board and committee members. Two offenders were also present to discuss how attending the programmes had affected them. In his speech at the launch, the Probation Centre manager stressed that four principles underlay the Probation Service's work: prevention of reoffending; protecting the public; reparation; and ensuring compliance and the rigorous and swift enforcement of orders.

Information packs were devised to ensure that comprehensive information on all community penalty options was available to sentencers when adjourning for reports and when passing sentence. These were distributed at the relaunch, and subsequently sent to all sentencers in the area. The packs included a calendar showing when courses of any type were running, so that sentencers could see at a glance when an offender might start and finish.

Each programme was described on a single A4 sheet. This information included the aims of the programme, how it worked, its length, the target group, how it might be accessed (including the words that needed to be added to the Probation Order) and the other programmes with which it might be combined. Two further brochures included in the pack provided more details of the statutory programmes as well as the aims and content of straight probation, information on the aims and content of CS and combination orders. This offending-focused work was carefully presented as distinct from social work-type interventions that were described separately, along with arrangements for dealing with mentally disordered offenders.

One imaginative suggestion for new work on CS was that a team should renovate the duck pond outside the courthouse in Middlesbrough. This was done. Otherwise, very few new ideas were proposed for improving the content of CS placements, probably because the Service already offered a range of work, from physically demanding tasks such a clearing forest paths to placements helping the elderly. However, the fact that a number of suggestions made by magistrates for new CS work were already available highlighted an important information gap. As a result the Probation Service put together a further information pack which explained the purpose of CS, described each of the 17 projects they operated including the type of work involved, start dates, duration, location and what benefits to the community they produced. Thus, sentencers were made more fully aware of what work was available on CS and could take that into account when passing sentence.

Dialogue between some sentencers and the senior probation staff, on questions such as whether offenders on CS should wear uniform, was also useful in enabling probation staff to explain how this might increase an offender's social exclusion and (thus) have an adverse effect on rehabilitation.

By late January 1997 the justices' clerks from Teesside and Hartlepool magistrates' courts had written to all members of Bench asking them to attend six hours of training about the changes being introduced. The training was carried out by the justices' clerks, a deputy clerk, the court manager, senior probation staff and senior magistrates, some of whom were also members of the LSG. The scale of their support for the project is indicated by the fact that 92 per cent of magistrates attended training over the next two months. Although no new training was deemed necessary for judges and recorders, the LSG sent them written details of what was being done locally and they were also briefed by the Resident Judge shortly before the official start of the project.

Comprehensive training packs were produced, based on material outlined by the National Steering Group, and distributed at the training sessions. These packs:

- explained the aims of the community sentence demonstration project;

- provided detailed information on the aims and content of locally available community sentences;

- clarified enforcement procedures; and

- described how sentencers could obtain aggregate information about the success of particular programmes.

The training sessions also made use of sentencing exercises which illustrated the changes being introduced.

Participants told the researchers attending one such session that they found the sentencing exercise particularly useful as it gave them a chance to think through the practical effects of the demonstration project on individual offenders. One consequence of this was that magistrates decided that they would like to make use of a checklist when requesting pre-sentence reports (PSRs) so that report writers were given a clearer idea about what the court wanted reports to cover.

The checklist is shown in Appendix A and detailed information on its use is provided in Chapter 5. However, it is worth noting here that the Teesside LSG discovered that magistrates often passed the checklist to defence solicitors to complete, partly because they felt that some topics should not be covered in open court and partly because they felt the solicitor would obtain a fuller, and perhaps more honest, response from the defendant. The Bench also completed an Adjournment for Pre-Sentence Report form (see Appendix B) which enabled them to record a preliminary indication of the seriousness with which they viewed the offence, note the main purpose(s) the sentence should serve (reparation, restriction of liberty, prevention of reoffending), and specify what additional requirements might be attached to a probation order[5]. Two other features of the form are particularly noteworthy – the Bench could recommend that the time spent being actively supervised should exceed the requirements of National Standards; and, in specifying the type of work to be done on CS, they could ask for forms of work not currently available to be considered. Again, information on the use of this form is presented in Chapter 5.

---

5   It was recognised that, as the bench of lay magistrates requesting the PSR were unlikely to be those using it in sentencing the offender, those indications should be non-binding. The form of words used was based on a draft prepared by the National Steering Group.

Initially, use of the forms appeared to be slowing down court business, as some magistrates felt that they should retire to discuss and complete the forms. However, as they became more familiar with the forms and the process, the LSG found that this problem was resolved.

Probation representatives at the LSG reported that the usefulness of the Adjournment for Pre-Sentence Report forms varied according to how well they had been completed. In some cases magistrates had ticked all options, whereas in others they had been very specific about the issues they wanted covered, and probation representatives on the LSG confirmed that report writers had found that very useful. The checklist also proved useful within the Probation Service, as an additional check on the quality of PSRs and as a way of ensuring that the programmes provided matched those required by sentencers.

Three months into the project, the LSG's own review of progress found that photocopies of the checklists and proformas were slow to reach the Probation Service. This potentially serious drawback to the new system for improving the focus of PSRs was overcome by the simple expedient of using self-carbonating forms.

A form of words for sentencing pronouncements was also agreed, based on a draft prepared by the National Steering Group. The LSG's three-month review showed that this was being used extensively by some magistrates, but not by all.

Given that one of the overall aims of the projects was to enhance public confidence in community sentences, we carried out a short but intensive period of observation to discover whether any of the new arrangements for requesting PSRs or pronouncing sentence in the magistrates' courts would be apparent to a member of the public. Over two and a half days during the last month of the project researchers sat in the public benches of the five busiest courtrooms in Teesside[6]. During that period, 152 cases were observed, of which eight resulted in adjournments for PSRs and nine resulted in a community sentence being imposed. In seven of the eight adjournment cases the impact of the new arrangements was apparent – in six cases the chair of the Bench commented on the seriousness of the offence and in four instances he or she also indicated what the main purpose of the sentence they were considering would be (eg reparation, restriction of liberty etc). In three of the four cases where checklists (Appendix A) had been completed, the Probation Service was asked to focus on particular difficulties highlighted on the checklist. In two cases the chair asked for the Probation Service to assess the offender's suitability for a particular form of

---

6   The researchers were prepared to spend up to five days in each area observing court proceedings, but as the first two and a half days only yielded 17 relevant cases, and cost over £1,600, the lead researcher decided to curtail the observation period. There is no reason to assume that the observation period was in any way untypical.

additional requirement (see Appendix B). In the eighth case the chair simply announced that 'the Probation Service will prepare a PSR to help the sentencing Bench'.

A checklist had been completed for all nine of the offenders whom the research team saw being sentenced to serve community penalties at Teesside magistrates' court. In seven of these cases the chair described the content of the sentence in terms of supervision requirement and/or courses and programmes the offender would have to attend. In six cases, it also spelt out clearly what would happen if the offender failed to comply with the order. The purpose of the sentence was only made explicit in one case, where the offender was convicted of stealing a chequebook and four other related offences. Imposing a 12-month probation order with a requirement to attend the 'Thinking Straight On Probation' course, as proposed in the PSR, the chairman said the order was intended to prevent reoffending.

The impact of the demonstration project at the Crown Court in Teesside was rather different to that at the magistrates' court. Checklists were not employed because most PSRs are prepared for Plea and Direction Hearings rather than in response to a request from a judge. However, judges made use of the opportunity to make more specific referrals to CS projects. They were also somewhat more likely to request feedback reports. By March 1998 the LSG found that while only seven specific requests for individual feedback were received from magistrates, there were 29 from the Crown Court.

Finally, it is worth noting that the Probation Service had been able to offer information on whether individual offenders had attended one-to-one supervision or programmes as required, and what breach action had been taken from the start of the project. They were also willing to generate such information for any of the programmes they ran. As a matter of course the Service already produced regular bulletins on caseloads and staffing.

Changes in Shropshire

The LSG for the community sentence demonstration project in Shropshire was also chaired by the Resident Judge. Other members were the stipendiary magistrate, chairs of two local Benches, the two justices' clerks, the chair of the probation committee and the Chief Probation Officer. Like the Teesside LSG, this group also met for the first time in late September 1996, when a number of reservations about the project were voiced. Magistrates were particularly concerned about the additional time they would have to spend in training for the project, although they were prepared to attend a short briefing event. Doubts were also raised about some of the aims of the project – for example, was feedback on an offender's progress during an order important when compared with subsequent reconviction? Despite this, the group agreed to the project going ahead and decided to invite the other Bench chairs onto the LSG.

By the time of the second meeting it had been agreed that the national aims of the project were too ambitious given the timescales and training requirements and that the project in Shropshire should focus on one of the aims: increasing confidence in the use of community sentences. A local action plan was devised on that basis. Ensuring compliance and dealing with breach were seen as the key issues in making community sentences credible. It was also subsequently agreed that non-binding indications of seriousness should be used by courts requesting PSRs. In fact, as the Teesside project had made such fast progress on this front, Shropshire decided simply to adopt their adjournment form (Appendix B), with some minor amendments to suit local circumstances. The LSG also agreed a form of words to be used in court when explaining to the offender why it was adjourning for reports (Appendix C), and for a sentencing pronouncement (Appendix D). Comprising five elements the pronouncement explained: why the offence was serious enough to merit a community penalty; any mitigating factors; the type and length of order; the nature of any additional conditions; and queries about the offender's understanding of what had been said and whether he/she was prepared to comply.

Plans were also made at the same meeting to cultivate better relationships with the local media, to appear on the local radio station to promote the project and to make a video about the content of community sentences in Shropshire (see below).

One dilemma facing the Shropshire LSG was whether to announce the project to sentencers throughout the area before making firm plans about exactly what it would encompass. They chose to wait, with the result that the first few months of designing and setting up the project in Shropshire was dogged by criticisms that the LSG was not keeping magistrates informed. However, it is not clear that making an earlier announcement would have been a better approach as it could easily have led to complaints that the LSG had nothing concrete to say.

Magistrates' resistance to the idea of fresh training resulted in short (one and a half hours) briefing sessions being set up instead. These were delivered by a justices' clerk, the Chief Probation Officer and an ACPO, and were attended by 124 magistrates (46%). The briefing covered much the same ground as the Teesside training but in much less depth and without the practical exercises.

By the end of March 1997 all the relevant maingrade probation staff had attended one of four half-day briefing events on responding to the new PSR guidance from sentencers.

A separate reception was held for local solicitors, the police and Crown Prosecution Service in March 1997. The reasons why this was so poorly attended are unclear, but may reflect the fact that these groups did not expect the project to affect them.

One month after the project officially began the LSG reviewed progress. At that time concerns were expressed about the whether magistrates were following advice that had been issued about providing clearer, more directive requests for PSRs, and making sentencing pronouncements. Three months into the project, concern was expressed about how little change was visible in practice at court. As in Teesside, researchers spent two and a half days observing court proceedings in four courtrooms at the busiest magistrates' court (Telford) towards the end of the project to discover what, if any, aspects of the changes introduced would be apparent to a member of the public. Forty-two appearances were observed, of which five were adjourned for PSRs to be prepared and resulted in a community sentence being imposed.

Elements of the new adjournment pronouncement (Appendix C) were used in three cases. In one case the chair stuck very closely to the written version of the pronouncement, including asking the Probation Service to consider the offender's suitability for an anger-management course. Relevant elements of the sentencing pronouncement (Appendix D) were used in all four of the sentenced cases observed.

While the demonstration project in Shropshire got off to a much slower start than that in Teesside, by autumn 1997 it had gained considerable momentum and a number of planned changes were implemented. First, the planned video on community sentences was issued. This covered the type of work available on CS and how offenders were supervised. It was aimed primarily at magistrates, although the accompanying brochure was intended for a wider circulation. The brochure covered most of the programmes listed in Table 2.3, and the opportunity was taken to stress that the assessment and management of risk were core elements of the work of the Service and to gently educate the reader about some of the difficulties offenders faced. It also covered: how probation orders operate, the different models of CS available and some examples of what CS participants had achieved; how partnership organisations help with accommodation problems, general advice on debt, benefits, relationship and family problems; specialist advice and assessment regarding employment and education; and the role played by forensic psychologists in assessing and supporting particular groups of offenders (eg sex offenders).

Second, one-page sheets were prepared for sentencers on CS, probation and combination orders and the aims, content and timing of five programmes available to offenders in Shropshire covering employability, anger-management, alcohol education, sex offending, and motoring education. These were designed to be routinely attached to any PSR in which they were proposed.

Third, the Probation Service arranged for magistrates to visit CS projects which, the LSG reported, they found both interesting and useful.

Fourth, special enforcement courts were introduced in Telford and Shrewsbury reducing the time between the issuing of a summons and court appearance to 14 days, from a previous average of six weeks.

Fifth, a public relations consultant was appointed to raise the profile of the project and of community sentencing, and sixth, the project was given more impetus and considerable local publicity when the then Minister for Probation, Joyce Quin, visited the area and met with members of the Local Steering Group.

Finally, a sign of the momentum the project had gained during the course of the year was that an end-of-project training event in February 1998 was attended by 200 of the 269 Shropshire magistrates, when the importance of building on developments during the course of the project was strongly supported.

3 Did sentencers change their views about community penalties?

In considering the effects of the changes the two Local sSeering Groups planned and implemented, it is important to know what sentencers thought about community penalties as the community sentence demonstration projects began and whether their views had changed by the end of the projects. We therefore examined changes in sentencers' views on a range of issues, including:

- the primary purpose of straight probation, probation with additional requirements, community service (CS), combination orders and custody;

- the information the Probation Service provided on the availability of probation programmes and CS projects;

- knowledge about the content of probation programmes and CS work;

- satisfaction with the range of additional requirements and types of CS work available locally;

- the value of pre-sentence reports (PSRs);

- the value of the needs checklists and adjournment forms in the 'after' period;

- the supervision and enforcement of community sentences;

- the need for feedback on individual offenders or on particular programmes.

Information on each of these topics was obtained in two ways. First, all lay magistrates in both areas were asked to complete a postal questionnaire as the demonstration projects began and then again as they ended.

In the 'before' period, we were able to 'piggyback' on the initial training sessions for magistrates in both areas by including the questionnaires in training/briefing packs. As 92 per cent of magistrates in Teesside attended the community sentence demonstration projects (CSDP) training sessions, the questionnaire response rate was correspondingly high, at 86 per cent. However, the equivalent attendance for the Shropshire CSDP 'briefing' was only 46 per cent, which meant that we had to rely far more heavily on the responses from those who received the questionnaire by post. This still produced a 68 per cent response rate. In the 'after' period, the questionnaires were not tied to training events and thus produced similar response rates to the latter figure (See Table 3.1).

Table 3.1: Response rates by Shropshire and Teesside magistrates in 'before' and 'after' periods

Area	Before (%)	Achieved (n)	After (%)	Achieved (n)
Teesside	86	325	69	245
Shropshire	68	184	67	178

There were no significant differences in the 'before' and 'after' samples for each area in terms of gender breakdown, time served on the Bench or the type of court proceedings the magistrates usually adjudicated over (eg adult vs youth court). This is unsurprising as those in the 'before' and 'after' samples were often the same people[7].

Table 3.2: Interviews with sentencers in Shropshire and Teesside in 'before' and 'after' periods

Area	Type of sentencer	Before (n)	After (n)
Teesside	Judges and Recorders[8]	7	7
	Chairmen of the Bench	4	-
Shropshire	Judges	1	1
	Chairmen of the Bench	6	-
	Stipendiary	1	-
Both areas	All sentencers	19	8

---

7   As the 'before' and 'after' samples were largely non-independent (ie the same magistrates often appeared in both), we considered only examining those results using paired t-tests. However, this would have meant ignoring the responses of magistrates who only participated in one stage or the other, which could have introduced bias. Instead, we chose to use chi-squared tests of significance, with significant results being checked using a two-tail z test to examine questions with a 'very/always' option. This set an unusually conservative standard for results to reach statistical significance as chi-squared assumes independent samples, whereas there is less likely to be variation in non-independent samples (because a magistrate in the 'before' sample who was very satisfied is unlikely to change to very dissatisfied in the 'after' sample). For a discussion of this type of approach, see Kish, L (1965). Finite population corrections were calculated and applied, although this only had an appreciable effect in Teesside in a few instances and none at all in Shropshire.

8   Four of the judges interviewed at each stage were the same individuals.

Second, as explained in Chapter 1, we also interviewed Crown Court sentencers and senior magistrates who were involved in the demonstration projects before the project began (see Table 3.2). Judges were also interviewed in the 'after' period. These interviews covered broadly the same ground as the postal questionnaires but provided much more detailed replies that were valuable in their own right and useful in interpreting the quantitative questionnaire data.

Did sentencers change their views about the purpose of community penalties ?

The postal survey asked magistrates to state what they saw as the main aims of: probation orders; probation orders with requirements; combination orders; community service orders; and custody. In the 'before' period sentencers in both areas thought that all probation orders, and to a lesser extent, combination orders, were primarily aimed at preventing further offending or rehabilitation. Consistent with previous research (Flood-Page and Mackie, 1998), very few magistrates (less than 5% in all cases) thought the main aim of probation was the restriction of liberty. In addition, less than half thought that such orders had any restrictive impact at all (as opposed to this being its main function).

Overall, as Tables 3.3a and 3.3b show, magistrates' opinions on the aims of most sentences changed very little, although there was a significant increase in the proportion of magistrates in both areas who thought that preventing reoffending was the main aim of probation orders with requirements. There was also an increase in the proportion who viewed this as the main aim of straight probation, although the change was only significant in Teesside[9]. In fact, there were some (non-significant) signs of a general increase in the power of all community penalties and of prison to prevent reoffending.

However, nearly half of respondents in both periods and in both areas continued to believe that the main purpose of CS was reparation; and the most commonly held view of prison was that it served mainly to keep offenders out of circulation. Interestingly, only one magistrate in each area in the 'before' period, and none in the 'after' period, thought that the primary aim of custody was to rehabilitate offenders. Indeed, in the 'before' interviews, the other sentencers noted that although there was scope for rehabilitation in prisons, they had little confidence that currently prisons were being run in a way which had a rehabilitative effect.

---

9   The probability that a 'statistically significant' difference occurred by chance is 5 per cent or less.

Table 3.3a: How Teesside magistrates' views about the main aims of community sentences and prison changed (%)

	Prevention of reoffending		Reparation		Restriction of liberty		Deterrence		Rehabilitation	
	Before	After	Before	After	Before	After	Before	After	Before	After
Probation	50	61	1.5	2	3	2	1.5	3	35	30
Probation + requirements	35	45	2	5	3	2	5	5	44	40
Combination order	32	38	14	15	14	12	12	11	17	19
Community service	18	19	40	46	17	22	10	9	7	2
Prison	15	17	1	1	57	65	17	14	0	0

Table 3.3b: How Shropshire magistrates' views about the main aims of community sentences and prison changed (%)

	Prevention of reoffending		Reparation		Restriction of liberty		Deterrence		Rehabilitation	
	Before	After	Before	After	Before	After	Before	After	Before	After
Probation	50	57	4	3	2	2	2	3	36	34
Probation + requirements	36	49	8	8	2	4	5	7	39	33
Combination order	35	43	18.5	16	9	8	15	10	12	17
Community service	16	26	47	47	11	12	12	7	4	7
Prison	12	17	0	0	59	70	21	12	0	0

Was there a change in sentencers' knowledge of the availability of probation programme and CS work places ?

One of the aims of the demonstration projects was to increase sentencer awareness of the availability of places on current probation programmes and of the different types of CS work on offer. The postal survey of magistrates shows that just over half of all magistrates in the 'before' period were satisfied with the information on the availability of places on probation programmes and that this improved significantly in the 'after' period (Shropshire from 51% to 64%; Teesside from 52% to 72%).

Two-thirds of the sentencers interviewed in the 'before' period (in both areas) were satisfied that they knew whether places were available on both probation programmes and CS orders. However, all interviewees noted that this was rarely an issue. If availability was not noted as a problem in the PSR they assumed that the offender would start the probation requirement or community service order immediately.

Those who were interviewed at the start of CSDP were also asked how quickly they expected offenders to start a specified activity after being sentenced. Their estimates varied considerably but the average was 20 days. However, none of them actually knew how long it took or requested information on start dates. Most assumed that the Probation Service would mention any delay in the PSR if this was a problem. Two Shropshire magistrates said that the Probation Service would stick to National Standards on this (Home Office, 1995), but did not know what the relevant standard specified. In fact, there is no national standard on this. In the 'after' period, four judges from Teesside said that they were usually told the start date of the requirement in PSRs, and two of them put this down to the impact of CSDP.

Did sentencers become more knowledgeable about the content of probation programmes and community service work?

As noted in Chapter 1, one of the main aims of CSDP was to make sentencers more aware of existing Probation Service provision. The postal survey showed that around three-quarters of magistrates in both areas already felt 'very' or 'fairly' well informed about probation programmes in the 'before' period. This was improved significantly in the 'after' period, to around 90 per cent. As most of the shift was accounted for by an increase in the number of magistrates who felt very well informed, it would seem that the projects fully met this particular objective.

Most of the sentencers interviewed before (15/19) and after the projects began (6/8) also felt very well informed about the probation programmes available in their areas both before and after the projects took effect, although the three recorders interviewed at both stages said they had not received either the information on probation programmes or the monthly updates on CS.

Sentencers in the 'before' period were less satisfied with the availability of information on the range of CS work available locally than on the range of probation options: only five of the 19 sentencers interviewed thought this was adequate before the demonstration project began. Judges in both Teesside and Shropshire thought that this had improved markedly in the 'after' period. The postal survey indicates that this situation significantly improved under CSDP in both areas, although less so in Shropshire than in Teesside. In Teesside, the relatively low proportion (40%) of magistrates who 'always' or 'frequently' felt they had enough information on community service placements increased to 70 per cent, whereas in Shropshire the change was from 31 per cent to 41 per cent.

Were sentencers satisfied with the range of additional requirements and CS work placements available locally?

Another objective of the demonstration projects was to discover whether sentencers were satisfied with the range of programmes available locally and to try to identify and fill any gaps in provision.

Probation programmes

The postal questionnaires revealed that magistrates in both areas felt significantly more confident that they could tailor sentences to individual offenders in the 'after' period. The percentage in Shropshire rose from 36 per cent to 54 per cent and that in Teesside increased from 40 per cent to 66 per cent. While all the eight judges interviewed at the end of the demonstration projects felt that their ability to tailor a sentence had improved, two still felt that they would like more direct influence on the content of probation orders for individual offenders, and four felt the same about community service orders. All the judges recognised, however, that there were practical limits to how far this could be achieved within existing resources.

The postal surveys show that around 30 per cent of magistrates in both areas thought that the range of probation programmes had increased since CSDP began. However, responses to questions about what these new programmes offered showed that they were actually much more informed about the range of *existing* programmes.

In fact, as noted in Chapter 2, there was little change in programme provision in either area, but both Probation Services had put considerable effort into making sentencers better informed about the range of programmes available. These results suggest that their efforts had been successful.

Community Service work

One-third of magistrates surveyed in Teesside, and one-quarter in Shropshire, thought that the range of CS work had increased during CSDP. Again, this largely reflected a better understanding of what was already available, although Teesside Probation Service had introduced some new types of work (see Chapter 2).

Three of the eight judges in the 'after' period would still have liked to change the type of CS work available, but did not agree on how the content should be changed. While one judge wanted to increase the placements that gave offenders responsibility for others, such as helping with the elderly or disabled, another wanted to see more:

'... *lifting, shovelling and dirty mucking about that makes them break into a sweat. They also need to be in uniform to increase the shame.*'

This same judge thought that CS tasks were still not well enough defined for sentencers to be able to specify the type of work offenders should do. He therefore suggested that PSRs should be very specific about the particular tasks an offender would carry out and how these related to specific aims, rather than leaving this to sentencers.

It is also noteworthy that, far from satisfying sentencers' demands, the demonstration projects increased the proportion of magistrates in both areas that would like to have additional CS work, probation programmes or combinations of order available to them. In Teesside the figure doubled from 23 per cent to 46 per cent (a statistically significant change). The change in Shropshire was not statistically significant (from 27% to 36%), but was in the same direction.

Were any of the options sentencers wanted not available within the current sentencing framework?

One of the main reasons the CSDPs were set up was to discover how far changes in community sentencing, consistent with the principles set out in the Green Paper *Strengthening Punishment in the Community* (Home Office, 1995) could be achieved within existing legislation (see Chapter 1). There is some evidence that, despite the changes Shropshire and Teesside Probation Services introduced to ensure that sentencers could tailor community sentences more closely to individual offenders, at least some of the sentencers interviewed would like to go further along this route than current legislation allows.

In the 'before' period, two judges wanted greater powers to combine different sentencing elements in a single disposal. One of the Shropshire magistrates also said he would like to be able to give offenders:

'... *a short taste of prison before being put on probation.*'

This view was shared by seven (2%) Teesside magistrates in the 'before' period postal survey. In the 'after' period, five of the eight judges interviewed argued along the following lines:

'We need to be able to use a deferred or suspended sentence or even a short prison sentence... followed by structured probation supervision, but more intensive than you get on licence.'

One of these judges gave as an example his desire to impose a short custodial sentence on a habitual driving offender for punishment, followed by the Probation Service's 'responsible driver' programme while on licence for rehabilitation.

The interviews suggested that most of the judges in the 'after' period felt frustrated by the limits of the sentencing options available to them, but this seemed to relate as much to a lack of confidence in prison's ability to rehabilitate, as it did to scepticism about community sentences' capacity to punish. As a result, Crown Court sentencers were casting around for something akin to American-style 'split sentencing', which involves imprisoning an offender for half the sentence length, with supervised release combined with home detention for the remaining portion of the sentence (see for instance, Klein-Saffran, 1992).

However, American research indicates that split sentences are associated with worse reconviction rates than most other forms of community sentence (Langan, 1994).

Apart from combining prison and probation, there were four other suggestions which sentencers believed would require legislation:

- one judge wanted a more flexible balance between probation and CS elements of combination orders; he felt that for some offenders it was more appropriate to make an order with a short probation element and a more substantial CS component – currently the probation element may be between one and three years and the CS element may be between 40 and 100 hours;

- two Shropshire magistrates suggested that it should be possible to offer reparation with a probation order by combining it with a fine and/or a compensation order – in fact, it is already possible to combine a community penalty with compensation, although not a fine, for a single offence;

- the same Shropshire magistrates also thought they should be able to stipulate the level of contact that must be maintained throughout an order[10];

- one judge wanted the option of community penalties combined with weekend custody or tagging[11].

---

10   Although these were suggestions for change, it is possible they simply did not know that this was covered by National Standards (see Ellis et al, 1996).
11   Currently, it is only possible to combine a community sentence with electronic monitoring in the three curfew order pilot areas.

The value of pre-sentence reports

Requesting PSRs

The postal survey showed that the changes introduced by the community sentence demonstration projects did not significantly change magistrates' attitudes toward PSRs (see Tables 3.4a and 3.4b). Around three-quarters of magistrates in both areas thought that a PSR was always necessary when considering a combination order or community service order. Slightly fewer thought that this was also true when imposing a probation order with additional requirements. Around 50 per cent to 60 per cent of magistrates in both areas thought that a PSR was always necessary when imposing straight probation. Most of the rest thought PSRs were sometimes useful and less than 3 per cent thought that reports were never necessary when imposing a community sentence.

Table 3.4a: Changes in Teesside magistrates' views on when PSRs are needed (%)

	Always		Sometimes		Rarely		Never	
	Before	After	Before	After	Before	After	Before	After
Probation order	48	52	39	36	8	7	2	3
Probation order with requirements	67	65	26	29	3	2	0	1
Combination order	77	72	19	24	1	1	0	0
Community service order	75	71	18.5	24	3	3	1	1
Custody	63	55	25	34	8	6	1.5	2

Table 3.4b: Changes in Shropshire magistrates' views on when PSRs are needed (%)

	Always		Sometimes		Rarely		Never	
	Before	After	Before	After	Before	After	Before	After
Probation order	58	53	32	37	8	6	0	1
Probation order with requirements	70	77	25	17	3	2	0	1
Combination order	80	81	16	15	2	>1	0	>1
Community service order	75	80	20	16	3	>1	0	>1
Custody	69	71	22	23	5	3	0	0

The ten lay magistrates interviewed said they always requested a PSR when considering a community penalty and seven said they would also do so when considering custody. Among the typical comments were:

'I want the Probation Service's agreement';

'You need a professional opinion';

and (for custody):

'A PSR satisfies me that there is no other option available.'

In contrast, only three[12] of the eight judges in the 'before' period said they always requested a PSR when considering community penalties or custody. However, this does not necessarily mean that they did not have PSRs available to them. Teesside Probation Service, for example, prepares PSRs in all guilty plea cases at the Crown Court; and recent research by Charles et al (1997) suggests that there is little difference in the extent to which the Crown Court and magistrates' courts dispense with PSRs.

The judges all remarked that they tried to avoid the 'time wasting and extra costs' caused by adjourning for PSRs, especially where the offender had a string of previous similar serious offences. In this sense, they argued, it was up to the defence counsel to convince them that offenders' circumstances were such that a PSR was essential. It should also be noted that both Probation Services had systems in place to provide same-day PSRs for the Crown Court (see Chapter 2).

The influence of PSRs

The postal survey showed that 75 per cent of magistrates in Teesside felt that PSRs influenced their choice of sentence and the proportion in Shropshire was even higher, at 85 per cent. The changes introduced under the CSDPs did not alter this significantly. Before the project began in Shropshire, 82 per cent of magistrates thought sentencing proposals were always or frequently appropriate. This did not significantly change in the 'after' period (84%). However, in Teesside the level of satisfaction was lower (70%) in the 'before' period, but improved significantly, to 77 per cent, in the 'after' period.

Three of the eight judges in the 'before' period and two different ones interviewed in the 'after' period said that PSRs rarely influenced their choice of sentence and that the proposals contained in such reports were rarely

---

12   Four of the eight judges in the 'after' period.

appropriate because they failed to reflect the seriousness of cases being dealt with at the Crown Court. In fact, even those who saw PSRs as influencing their decision tended to see community penalty disposals as 'taking a calculated risk' and whether they took such a risk depended on their opinion of the report writer:

> *'They err on the side of leniency. It depends on the individual reporter. Some are excellent and I respect and trust them. I only take a chance with these';*

and:

> *'I go out on a limb for a PSR writer I trust and know'.*

In considering whether PSRs should propose custody, the Home Affairs Committee (1998: xxxi, 107) concluded that:

> *'Although it may not be the case that pre-sentence reports never propose custodial sentences, it remains the case that they rarely do so explicitly. We recommend that National Standards be amended so that pre-sentence reports not only have to make it clear where non-custodial sentences have been considered inappropriate, but that they state explicitly that "a custodial option appears to be the only option available to the court' or words to that effect."*

Just over one-third (three magistrates, four judges) of the sentencers interviewed before the demonstration projects began and four of the eight judges interviewed in the 'after' period said that their confidence in PSR proposals would be improved if the writers were more willing to propose custody[13]. However, they also said that they did not feel very strongly about this and that generally they would be happy for PSR writers to offer no proposal as a proxy for custody, provided they refrained from proposing community penalties inappropriately[14]:

> *'I had a proposal for a combination order for someone caught with seven grams of heroin. I imposed four years custody.'*

Also, five sentencers did not see any merit in moving to explicit proposals for custody, with one judge commenting that he was:

> *'Happy with the coded message approach to custody proposals.'*

---

13 We did not ask about proposing custody in the postal survey for sentencers.
14 Figures from Teesside Probation Service's quarterly report for April-June 1997 show that over 90 per cent of PSRs with no proposal resulted in a custodial sentence. In contrast to one critic's claim 'it is interesting that the Probation Service never recommends a prison sentence' (evidence to the Home Affairs Committee, 1998, xxxi, 108), the Teesside figures also show that eight proposals were made for custody, all of which resulted in custody.

Taken together, these comments suggest that judges have differing views on the usefulness and appropriateness of PSRs. This makes it difficult to identify a single strategy Probation Services might employ to increase the influence of PSRs on Crown Court sentencing. It does, however, endorse the current practice of treating Crown Court work as a specialism; first, because this enables report writers to build up the sorts of relationships with judges which will encourage them 'take a chance' and use a community penalty; and second, because PSR writers need to recalibrate their proposals to fit the range of sentencing options judges use, which is much narrower and more weighted towards custody than that used by magistrates (which is the range with which most probation officers will be familiar).

Overall, it would seem that magistrates value PSRs and are heavily influenced by the sentencing proposals they contain. On the other hand, judges seemed to believe that they were often dealing with such serious cases that custody was a default option. In these cases they were only steered away from using custody when the report was written by a probation officer they knew and respected. It is of course true that some of the cases dealt with at the Crown Court are more serious than those sentenced by magistrates, but it is also true that many of the triable-either-way cases which reach the Crown Court could have been dealt with by magistrates and would have been within the non-custodial range of seriousness (Hedderman and Moxon, 1992).

Needs checklists and PSR adjournment forms

As noted in Chapter 2, needs checklists were introduced in Teesside while adjournment forms were introduced in both Teesside and Shropshire, as part of the demonstration projects. Both changes were popular, with 77 per cent of Shropshire magistrates and 91 per cent of Teesside magistrates indicating that they always or frequently used them. In both areas around three-quarters of magistrates who used the new forms agreed that they were useful. For example, one commented in interview that:

> 'Initially CSDP slowed down requests for PSRs, but now magistrates are used to it they are much quicker'.

One of the few who were less pleased with the new forms was concerned that:

> 'CSDP creates more work in court and as a result there is a tendency to go for custody in order to avoid the palaver'.

Sentencers' satisfaction with community sentence supervision

From the postal survey (see Tables 3.5a and 3.5b), it is clear that magistrates in both areas felt significantly better informed about supervision arrangements for all orders in the 'after' period. In Shropshire this coincided with a significant improvement in satisfaction with the supervision arrangements for all types of order in the 'after' period. In Teesside, although magistrates were generally more satisfied with supervision arrangements in the after period, this was only significant for probation orders with requirements and combination orders (see Tables 3.6a and 3.6b).

Table3.5a: Changes in Teesside magistrates' views on how well informed they felt about current supervision arrangements (%)

	Always		Sometimes		Rarely		Never	
	Before	After	Before	After	Before	After	Before	After
Probation order	8	14	53	60	33	22	3	2
Probation order with requirements	8	15	50	58	36	22	3	2
Combination order	5	11	43	60	44	22	3	2
Community service order	8	14	42	55	41	25	5.5	3

Table 3.5b: Changes in Shropshire magistrates' views on how well informed they felt about current supervision arrangements

	Always		Sometimes		Rarely		Never	
	Before	After	Before	After	Before	After	Before	After
Probation order	20	30	47	52	29	15	2	1
Probation order with requirements	12.5	26	50.5	53	32	19	2	1
Combination order	11	23	43.5	48	41	25	2	2
Community service order	14	25	40	48	40	24	3	2

Table 3.6a: Changes in Teesside magistrates' views on how satisfactory they considered community sentence supervision (%)

	Always		Sometimes		Rarely		Never	
	Before	After	Before	After	Before	After	Before	After
Probation order	13	20	63	61	11	7	1	1
Probation order with requirements	13	21	65	64	9	5	1	0
Combination order	12	16	65	69	9	4	1	>1
Community service order	15	18	62	65	10	5	1	>1

Table 3.6b: Changes in Shropshire magistrates' views on how satisfactory they considered community sentence supervision (%)

	Always		Sometimes		Rarely		Never	
	Before	After	Before	After	Before	After	Before	After
Probation order	19	32	59	57	3	1	0	0
Probation order with requirements	17	29	61	60	3	0	0	0
Combination order	11	23	65	67	5	0	0	0
Community service order	15	26	59	61	6.5	3	>1	0

Seven of the eight judges and ten of the 11 magistrates interviewed in the 'before' period thought that offenders were breached after a maximum of two unacceptable absences in line with National Standards (1995). One noted that he expected offenders on CS orders to be given more leeway, while another thought this should be the case for those on combination orders or on probation orders with requirements. The two sentencers who did not think offenders were breached according to National Standards had contrasting views. One (from Teesside) believed that:

'You can't do everything by the book. Breach officers have my trust';

whereas the other (from Shropshire) held that the Probation Service was reluctant to follow the Standards:

'... partly because it was an admission of failure'.

In the 'after' period, five of the eight judges interviewed thought that the Probation Service was slow to breach offenders and they were also critical of other aspects of enforcement practices. However, most of the criticism of enforcement related to court procedures rather than Probation Service action. For example, one judge commented that he had asked the Probation Service to inform him if an offender he had sentenced breached the order as he felt he could not rely on the magistrates' court to provide this information quickly enough.

Six of the eight judges interviewed at the end of the project thought that offenders sentenced at the Crown Court should come straight back to the Crown Court for breach hearings, as they felt magistrates were too willing to let an order continue and tended only to refer cases back to the Crown Court when they considered revocation was appropriate.

Requesting and receiving feedback

The recent Home Affairs Committee on Alternatives to Prison Sentences stated:

> *'We believe it is essential for sentencers to be aware of the results of the sentences they make in terms of their success, or otherwise, in preventing offenders from reoffending. Without such knowledge they remain ignorant of the effectiveness of the various sentencing options available to them.'* (Home Affairs Committee, 1998: xxxviii, 139)

In the same report, the National Association for the Care and Resettlement of Offenders (NACRO) argued that:

> *'If sentencers' confidence in community sentences is to be increased, it is important that they receive more systematic feedback on the success of individuals whom they and their colleagues have sentenced and on the overall success rates of local community supervision programmes'* (Home Affairs Committee, 1998: xxxviii, 137)

At first sight, CSDP produced rather paradoxical findings on sentencers' attitudes to feedback from the Probation Service, as did earlier research (May, 1995). The postal survey in both areas showed the proportion of magistrates who 'frequently' or 'always' requested such feedback never rose above 10 per cent in the 'before' or 'after' period, despite the fact that between 80 per cent and 90 per cent of magistrates said they would find such information useful. Interviews yielded a similar overall response; however, further questioning on this point revealed that this was because sentencers were only interested in receiving feedback on the progress of *individual* offenders when they felt they had taken a risk in sentencing (usually by using a community sentence rather than custody). Two judges commented that they still received individual feedback reports, from other jurisdictions, on *all* cases they had sentenced to community orders. They noted that these were usually unproblematic cases which they could not remember and the feedback was 'neither useful nor welcome'.

The magistrates interviewed in Teesside explained that they never requested such information, partly because they obtained it informally through regular contact with the Probation Service and partly because such information was available through the Probation Liaison Committee.

It became clear in discussion that most judges and magistrates would welcome aggregate data on success levels for particular programmes or types of community sentence[15].

---

15   Two judges in Teesside, in both 'before' and 'after' periods said they would have no use for such information and did not wish to receive it.

According to the postal survey, less than one-fifth of magistrates in each area 'always' or 'frequently' received feedback on programme performance before or after CSDP, although again, around 80 per cent to 90 per cent said they would find this useful. The three most commonly suggested forms this information should include were:

- reconviction/reoffending rates;

- changes in offenders' attitudes to offending; and

- programme attendance and completion rates.

Some respondents also wanted information on offenders' views about the programmes they attended; changes in the content of programmes; and changes in offenders' lifestyles.

Two of the 11 magistrates who said in interview that they had received feedback considered that it had subsequently (positively) affected their decision to use that programme. One of these commented that more systematic and regular feedback on CS would also increase her confidence in using that disposal.

When asked about the type of information they received, four said they received completion and re-offending updates during an order, but others were more vague, referring to general information in annual reports or anecdotal information from informal feedback. However, when asked about the type of feedback they would *like* to see, most sentencers were much more specific. They were particularly concerned to know about changes in attitude or behaviour as a key measure of success, and some also mentioned long-term reconviction figures.

The responses to the postal questionnaires and the interviews suggest that that sentencers tend to be unaware of the types of measure Probation Services are likely to be able to offer, for example:

> *'Surely you can't do psychological tests on offenders to see if they've changed their attitudes?'*;

and:

> *'I would like reconviction information but don't know where to get it. I don't want it just for the local area, I need the relative success rate'.*

This indicates that sentencers would be more demanding in requesting programme level information if they were made more aware of the potential availability of outcome measures from standard instruments already used by many Probation Services, such as Offender Group Reconviction Scale (OGRS) (which can be used to compare two-year reconviction rates with their expected levels), CRIME-PICS II (which measures changes in attitudes to offending), and Level of Service Inventory - Revised (LSI-R) or Assessment, Case Recording and Evaluation System (ACE) which can be used to score changes in an offender's social problems and response to supervision.

Key findings

Comparing sentencers' opinions before and after the demonstration projects took place indicates that the projects were generally thought to have had a positive effect. In particular:

- the proportion of magistrates who saw probation with additional requirements as primarily concerned with the prevention of reoffending increased significantly during the demonstration period;

- the same change occurred in relation to straight probation in Teesside;

- views on other sentences were not significantly affected – CS continued to be seen as mainly a means by which offenders could put something back into the community (reparation); combination orders were seen as preventing reoffending; and prison as incapacitative;

- satisfaction with the information they had about the content and number of places on CS and probation programmes increased;

- magistrates in both areas became more confident that they could tailor sentences to individual offenders (although this was mainly a consequence of receiving better information about existing programmes);

- a minority of sentencers would like to be able to combine sentences in new ways (the most popular combination was mixing a short period of custody with community penalties);

- the majority of magistrates in both areas were 'always' or 'frequently' influenced in their choice of sentence by PSRs and most thought that PSR proposals were generally appropriate. In contrast, judges said they were rarely swayed by a PSR proposal; when they were, it was because they knew and respected the report's author;

- most magistrates welcomed the introduction of checklists, which caused PSR writers to focus on particular issues, and adjournment forms, which indicated sentencers' views on the seriousness of a case and the sorts of sentence they were leaning towards;

- sentencers in the 'after' period felt significantly better informed about supervision arrangements for all types of community order than in the 'before' period; satisfaction with the supervision of all community penalties improved in Shropshire's magistrates' courts but in Teesside the change was only significant in the case for probation orders with requirements and combination orders;

- only five of the eight Crown Court sentencers expressed satisfaction with the way orders were enforced in the 'after' period, compared with seven in the 'before' period; partly they were concerned about probation officers being too slow to take breach action, but their comments also concerned aspects of the magistrates' court process that were beyond the control of the probation service;

- the finding that the majority of sentencers wanted feedback in individual cases, but that most never asked for any, seems contradictory; however, it probably reflects the fact that they do not want this information on every individual they sentence, but on the few where they are particularly concerned about an offender's progress (often because they were considering custody but 'took a chance' on using a community penalty). Sentencers would welcome aggregated data on all offenders, however, in order to better judge the value of individual programmes and types of order.

4 Were the projects valuable from a probation perspective?

The interviews and postal surveys discussed in Chapter 3 were designed to discover what sentencers thought would make community sentences more credible and usable in the 'before' period and how far the projects had succeeded in these respects in the 'after' period. The probation officers' interviews and questionnaires, discussed in this chapter, focused on how the demonstration projects had affected their working practices and how far they saw the changes which had been introduced as beneficial or detrimental. Thus, probation staff were interviewed and asked to complete questionnaires *only* in the 'after' period.

The postal questionnaire was sent to all the 71 probation staff in Teesside and 43 in Shropshire who were directly involved in working with offenders in the community. After sending out one reminder letter, the overall response rate was 83 per cent. The characteristics of those who responded are shown in Table 4.1.

Table 4.1: *Characteristics of those returning questionnaires*

	Teesside	Shropshire	Both areas
No sent questionnaires	71	43	114
No returning questionnaires	58	37	95
Response rate (per cent)	82	86	83
Grades			
Senior Probation Officer	9	4	14%
CS Manager	1	0	11%
Probation Officer	39	28	71%
CS Officer	3	3	8%
Probation Service Officer	6	2	6%
Proportion – female (per cent)	55	49	53
Average length of service (range 1-29 years)	9 years	15 years	11 years

In addition, interviews were carried out with the key personnel in each area who were most closely involved in the project. In Teesside these included the Chief Probation Officer and three Assistant Chief Officers (ACO), the three Senior Probation Officers (SPOs) responsible for the probation centre, the magistrates' court team and servicing the Crown Court, and a community service (CS) manager. In Shropshire, the Chief and one ACO were interviewed as well as the two SPOs responsible for the magistrates' court team and CS and the two responsible for the Shrewsbury and Telford field teams.

Questionnaires and interviews included questions around seven main themes:

- the primary purpose of different community sentences and custody;

- contact with sentencers;

- the impact of the community sentence demonstration project (CSDP) inside the Service;

- the value of pre-sentence reports (PSRs) and the role of needs checklists and adjournment forms;

- changes in the supervision and enforcement of community sentences;

- the provision of feedback on individual offenders or on particular programmes;

- views about what the project had achieved and what it had failed to achieve.

The aims of sentencing

As Table 4.2 shows, 80 per cent[16] of the probation staff who completed the questionnaire considered that the main aim of a straight probation order or a probation order with additional requirements was to reduce reoffending. This compares with 59 per cent of magistrates from both areas in the 'after' period (see Chapter 3). Probation with additional requirements was the only sentence where rehabilitation was considered to be the main aim by more than 10 per cent of respondents (compared with 37% of magistrates). Less than 3 per cent of probation respondents thought that the main aim of either order was to deter, and no one thought they provided reparation or restriction of liberty. The percentage of magistrates who considered these to be the main aims of probation with or without requirements was similarly low.

---

16   In this chapter, the results from both areas are averaged when discussing the postal survey results unless this would be misleading (i.e. where staff in one area report quite different views to the other).

There was a less clear-cut view of the aim of combination orders and CS among probation staff. For example, while more than two-thirds of respondents thought combination orders were mainly intended to prevent reoffending, 10 per cent thought they were mainly a method of providing reparation and 10 per cent thought they were mainly intended to restrict liberty. While many magistrates (40%) agreed that the main aim of a combination order was the prevention of reoffending, rehabilitation was the second most commonly cited aim in both areas (18%), followed by reparation (15%).

Nearly three-quarters of probation respondents saw the main aim of prison as being restriction of liberty (incapacitation), although 15 per cent thought it was mainly intended as a deterrent. No one thought its main aim was to rehabilitate. The results discussed in Chapter 3 suggest that magistrates seemed to view custody in much the same way.

Table 4.2: **The main aims of community sentences and prison from a probation perspective (N=95)* (%)**

	Prevention of reoffending	Reparation	Restriction of liberty	Deterrence	Rehabilitation
Probation	83	-	-	1	10
Probation + requirements	80	-	-	2	13
Combination order	65	10	10	5	5
Community service	10	66	19	1	1
Prison	5	-	74	15	-

*   Rows may not sum to 100 per cent because up to 6 per cent of respondents did not express a view

The extent and quality of contact with sentencers

Probation staff completing the postal questionnaires in both areas said they usually came into contact with sentencers at court (90%), while less than half said they had never met a sentencer during a probation centre visit. Most respondents said that the demonstration project had not affected the frequency with which they came into contact with sentencers, although 11 per cent said the frequency of contact had increased at probation centres and 13 per cent said contact had increased at open days since the projects began. All but one interviewee in Shropshire also claimed that contact had increased, although most of those interviewed in Teesside thought there had only been a slight change because contact levels had always been high.

When asked about the quality of their relationships with sentencers:

- 78 per cent said their knowledge about the sorts of disposals sentencers were considering had improved;

- 73 per cent felt that their understanding of what sentencers wanted to know about offenders had increased;

- 20 per cent of those who said there had been no change felt that this was because it was not needed; and

- One Teesside respondent thought the demonstration project had detrimentally affected relationships with sentencers[17].

The impact of the projects within the Probation Service

The main impact of the projects on work *within* the Probation Service was that 54 per cent of those who responded to the survey reported an improvement in the timeliness and quality of information on the range and content of programmes available. The rest said this had not changed (of whom one-third thought no change was needed).

One-fifth of Shropshire respondents and one-quarter of those in Teesside thought liaison between court-based and field staff had improved. The Teesside respondent who thought the project had adversely affected relationships with sentencers, thought that the same was true of relationships within the Service. A majority of respondents in both areas (71%) thought this relationship was unchanged (just under half of these also said there was no need for improvement).

While just over half of respondents in both areas thought the projects had not affected their workloads, in Shropshire the remainder (46%) thought their workload had increased, whereas in Teesside 34 per cent probation staff thought their workload had increased and 12 per cent thought it had decreased. Of those who said the project had caused them more work, 12 mentioned an increase in orders with additional requirements, 14 mentioned the need to carry out more tailored PSRs and six mentioned a rise in requests for PSRs. Other factors mentioned were training and meetings (six) and administration (five). Three of the seven respondents in Teesside who said their workload had decreased said that they were being asked to supervise fewer CS orders. The others did not give an explanation.

---

17   Where a single Teesside respondent is reported as having negative views about different aspects of CSDP, it is worth noting that this was the same respondent in all cases.

The value of pre-sentence reports and the role of needs checklists and adjournment forms

Around 90 per cent of those surveyed thought that a PSR was essential in all cases when probation orders with or without requirements or combination orders were being considered, and 70 per cent believed this to be essential when considering CS or prison. The others believed this was generally advisable but not essential, with the exception of one Teesside respondent who thought PSRs were rarely necessary.

One-third of those completing questionnaires in both areas said they saw some merit in PSR writers being prepared to propose custody and two-thirds did not. Those in favour commonly cited public safety and risk of reoffending, and the gravity of individual cases, but the most commonly given reason (in 13 cases) was that this would increase sentencers' confidence in PSRs. Eighteen of those who did not believe that PSRs should ever propose custody were prepared to acknowledge explicitly that there was sometimes no other choice but felt that this did not mean that they should positively propose custody. Six opposed it because they felt it would be 'pure window dressing' (because sentencers already knew custody was an option). However, half (30) of all those who opposed the idea of PSRs proposing custody said that this was because they felt it was their duty to make a positive recommendation for a measure they thought might be actively rehabilitative and they did not believe custody had any beneficial effects.

Most (12/14) of the probation staff interviewed from both areas were in favour of PSRs proposing custody, but an Assistant Chief Probation Officer (ACPO) in each area suggested that this should be restricted to reports written for the Crown Court where the caseload was serious enough to justify such a move.

Overall, 44 per cent of those responding to the postal survey thought that the targeting of PSR sentencing proposals had improved since the projects began and 40 per cent thought that the clarity of PSRs had improved. About half the remainder felt that the lack of change reflected the fact that PSR proposals and the clarity of PSRs required no improvement.

Only those who attended court regularly were asked in the postal survey about the way the sentencing process had changed and the use of checklists and Adjournments for Pre-Sentence Report forms. Seventeen of those who attended court in Shropshire (N=21) and 19 of those in Teesside (N=26), felt that the improvement in PSRs was associated with clearer indications from sentencers about what they wanted reports to cover. However, three of the probation staff interviewed in Teesside also suggested that a separate PSR quality assurance exercise, that had begun before the CDSP, had also contributed to this improvement.

Of the 26 probation staff who regularly attended court in Teesside, 21 said the checklist was used frequently and three said it was used occasionally (two respondents did not answer this question). Eighteen of the 26 said they found the checklist useful for a variety of reasons but mostly it helped them to tailor PSRs (nine) and to narrow the field of inquiry (four). Five said they did not find the checklist helpful. Only two of the remaining three respondents said that the checklists were too superficial and general to be useful.

Fourteen of the 17 respondents in Teesside who said that the adjournment proforma was in regular or occasional use thought it was helpful and three did not. Reasons for it being helpful included providing guidance on how seriously the court viewed the case (three) and the sort of sentence it had in mind (four). Three also suggested that it encouraged magistrates to treat cases more consistently.

Of the 21 Shropshire respondents who attended court regularly, eight said that Adjournment for Pre-Sentence Report forms were always used and 11 said they were used frequently. Again, a majority (14) found these forms helpful for similar reason to those offered in Teesside. One interviewee suggested that the forms main value lay in 'opening up a dialogue' between PSR writers and sentencers, and another saw it as something which PSRs should not simply follow but use creatively:

> '...take the germ of sentencers' ideas and pick up key themes.'

Only two of the respondents from Teesside and Shropshire who did not find the adjournment proformas helpful gave reasons for this. One said that he thought *his* view of the seriousness of an offence and which sentence might be appropriate was far more important than that of the Bench adjourning for reports. The other felt that a proper consideration of how serious the offence was and the appropriate sentence should wait until after the PSR was prepared because that would present an impartial account of events, whereas at adjournment all the court would have to go on was the prosecution's portrayal of events.

One of the ways in which the demonstration projects were expected to enhance the credibility of community sentences was by making sentencing pronouncements clearer so that offenders were told why they were being sentenced in particular ways, and the implications of non-compliance. However, over half (13) of the Shropshire staff who regularly attended court said this rarely or never happened, as did slightly less than half (11) of those in Teesside. This is in line with the results of our own periods of smallscale observation in Teesside and Telford magistrates' courts described in Chapter 2.

Changes in supervision and enforcement

All those interviewed and completing questionnaires were asked about the range of methods they regularly employed to improve compliance before *and* after the demonstration projects began. Two officers from Teesside said they made greater use of written and oral explanations of supervision requirements, but less use of appointment cards and diaries and arranging appointments to coincide with significant events (eg 'signing on'). It seems unlikely that these changes were made as a result of the demonstration project. For all other respondents, there was no change at all. New techniques introduced during the demonstration project in Teesside included interviewing offenders before they began programmes and improving the speed with which offenders were seen after a community order was imposed. (No new techniques were mentioned by Shropshire respondents.)

As Table 4.3 shows, there was considerable variation in the extent to which different techniques for ensuring compliance were used in the two project areas.

Table 4.3: ***Techniques for ensuring compliance during the demonstration projects***

	Teesside (%)	Shropshire (%)
Explanation of supervision and attendance requirements	93	84
Appointments timed to coincide with other significant events	86	68
Appointments cards or diaries	57	62
Unannounced and pre-arranged home visits	90	35
Incentives (eg outdoor pursuits)	53	8
N	58	37

Respondents in each area also said they used techniques for dealing with breach to a different extent before and after the projects began (see Table 4.4). The main change in Teesside was in the use of special breach courts, whereas Shropshire respondents reported that the speed with which breach cases were brought to court had improved (although they seemed unaware that this was achieved through the use of special breach courts).

There was no shortage of suggestions from either area about how compliance rates might be improved, including:

• making the breach process faster (14 respondents);

- simplifying the process (13 respondents);

- being more willing to breach (six respondents); and

- making the requirements of orders clearer to an offender at the start of an order (four respondents).

In line with the findings of previous research into probation officers' views on enforcement (Ellis et al, 1996), interviewees also commented that breach sometimes resulted from offenders being given sentences that were too demanding. For example, one SPO said that PSR writers could be more aware of this when recommending orders with additional requirements.

Table 4.4: **Techniques for dealing with breach during demonstration projects**

	Teesside		Shropshire	
	Before	After	Before	After
	%	%	%	%
Home visits to follow up breach	67	69	3	3
Faster hearing dates	47	41	22	32
Special breach courts	79	90	56	56
Specialist breach officers	71	72	35	38
N	58		37	

Percentages are shown for ease of comparison, but it should be noted that small number changes can result in large percentage changes.

When asked about the extent to which sentencers requested information about breach rates, one respondent in each area said such requests had increased at the Crown Court and three said they had increased at the magistrates' courts in Teesside.

Feedback on individual offenders or particular programmes

Probation staff in both areas said that requests for feedback on individual offenders were rare. For example, five officers (14%) in Shropshire and 16 (28%) in Teesside said they had *never* been asked for such information by magistrates, yet only one or two from each area said they would have any difficulty in providing it. Most respondents and interviewees said that requests for such information had neither increased nor decreased since the demonstration projects began, although 14 said there had been a discernible increase in such requests at the Teesside magistrates' courts.

Requests for feedback about programmes was more common. In this instance only one or two respondents in each area had noticed a change in the extent to which such information was requested. Once again, few respondents saw any difficulty in providing such information if it was requested, although one said he did not think that programmes were well enough monitored to provide very detailed information about success in terms of reconviction as opposed to attendance levels.

The probation staff who were interviewed were asked to comment on the fact that the sentencer survey showed they were keen to receive feedback on individuals and programmes but that the postal survey of probation staff showed they were rarely asked to provide it. Senior managers in both areas described a number of steps they had taken to try to provide such information more routinely (without being asked for it). For example, probation notice boards had been set up in Shropshire courts and the Service had offered sentencers more opportunities to visit schemes where they would have a chance to discuss completion rates etc with staff. Most of those interviewed said they had tried as many different techniques as they could think of to give magistrates such information.

Achievements and failures

Three-quarters of probation staff in Teesside who responded to the questionnaire said they had attended training specifically about the CDSP. The amount of training varied considerably but averaged ten hours. Six of the eight Teesside staff who were interviewed thought that the additonal training available for probation staff had been appropriate, the other two thought it had been too basic. All five of those who had been involved in the delivery of training to magistrates felt that the content and amount of training had been generally suitable, although some concern was expressed about the lack of focus on issues such as suitability and risk.

In Shropshire, 60 per cent of respondents said they had attended training and the average amount of training was four hours. Three of the six Shropshire interviewees were able to comment on training for probation staff. One of these thought it had been superficial, the others thought it had been appropriately pitched. Only one of the five who had been involved in the magistrates' briefing thought this had been adequate. It had given them a better understanding of the local community sentence options.

Among the other positive effects respondents attributed to the CDSP, 17 said it had not only improved sentencers' awareness of programmes but also the extent to which they made use of programmes. Eleven said the project had improved their relationship with sentencers, and nine had found the more directive information received from sentencers through the checklist (Appendix A) and adjournment information (Appendix B) useful. One of the senior officers interviewed in Shropshire also thought the project had been useful in highlighting gaps in provision – such as hostels and projects for women offenders.

Thirty-nine (41%) probation staff felt that despite the impact of the project there was still a lot of work to be done, particularly in improving probation/sentencer communication (N=13) and sentencer training (N=12).

Fifteen (26%) respondents from Teesside and 11 (30%) from Shropshire said that they felt the projects had negative effects: seven of the comments from Shropshire concerned the extra work the project had generated, PSRs taking longer and more PSRs being generated. The other comments reflected a belief that sentences had become *less* appropriate because sentencers were being more directive about on what they wanted a PSR to focus, rather than keeping an open mind until they received the PSR. In Teesside one respondent complained about extra work. The others expressed disquiet about its impact on sentencing, particularly that it was leading to less well-targeted sentencing and that sentencers might be 'overusing' additional requirements.

Two of those interviewed in each area were concerned that the scope of the demonstration projects had been too limited in that they had focused on what happened in court at the expense of addressing supervision and enforcement issues. Also, one of the senior managers in Teesside expressed concern about an increase in the number of additional requirements and the extra cost these imposed on the service. However, despite these reservations, all of those interviewed in both areas were otherwise very positive about the impact of the projects. One described it as 'a critical improvement'. Another summed up his response as:

> '... there is a commitment to make it work, to learn the lessons and extend into future practice. There were some early tensions, but these were surmountable, and it was certainly worthwhile.'

Key findings

The results of the postal survey and interviews with probation service staff suggest that:

- like magistrates, a majority of the Probation Staff surveyed saw the main aim of prison as being restriction of liberty (incapacitation); no one thought its main aim was to rehabilitate;

- four out of five probation staff, compared with three out of five magistrates, thought that the main aim of a straight probation order or a probation order with additional requirements was to reduce reoffending; as with magistrates, Probation Service views about the aims of combination orders and CS were less clear cut;

- the project seemed to have had more of an impact on the quality, rather than the frequency, of probation/sentencer contact;

- just over half the probation staff surveyed said that the project had also led to more timely and useful information being available on the range and content of programmes;

- over 40 per cent thought that the targeting of PSR sentencing proposals had improved since the projects began. Those who attended court saw this as related to the use of the checklists and adjournment forms, although three Teesside staff in interview ascribed the change to another initiative which had begun prior to CSDP;

- around half of those who regularly attended court said offenders were still rarely told why they were being sentenced in particular ways and the implications of non-compliance;

- the techniques used to promote compliance in either area seem to have been largely unaffected by the demonstration projects;

- most of those interviewed said they had tried as many different techniques as they could think of to give magistrates feedback information;

- CSDP training was seen as useful, although some of those interviewed were concerned that the training had not been focused enough on issues such as suitability and risk;

- overall, the positive effects of the project identified by those working in the two Services were: an increased use of probation programmes; improved relationships with sentencers; and a better understanding of what sentencers wanted PSRs to concentrate on. An increase in PSRs, with each one taking longer to prepare, and *less* appropriate sentencing were seen as the negative consequences of CSDP.

5 How did sentencing change?

Clearly, sentencers (especially magistrates) and the Probation Services in both areas considered that the demonstration projects had largely positive effects. This is important in itself, but a number of key questions remain about whether, and how, changes in procedure and attitudes affected sentencing. These include:

- in what ways did sentencing change?

- were these changes unique to the project areas?

- how were they related to the offences for which offenders were convicted?

- how far did sentencing decisions reflect pre-sentencing report (PSR) proposals?

- to what extent did PSR sentencing proposals reflect sentencers' views (as shown on adjournment forms) about offence seriousness?

To address these questions, data were collected and analysed on all cases sentenced at the Crown Court and magistrates' courts in the project areas for a six-month period before the projects began and for the same length of time towards the end of the demonstration projects (see Chapter 1). Comparative information was also obtained from Home Office RDS statistical databases about sentencing in the rest of England and Wales.

In what ways did sentencing change in the project areas?

At the Crown Court in Teesside, despite a 33 per cent increase in business, there was no significant change in the overall proportion of offenders receiving a discharge, fine, community penalty or a prison sentence (see Table 5.1). At the magistrates' courts in Teesside, where business rose by 22 per cent, there was a significant change in the use of community penalties, which accounted for 26 per cent of sentences in the 'before' period but only 21 per cent after the demonstration project began. To some extent this decline was offset by a (non-significant) increase in the use of fines, discharges and 'other' penalties such as compensation orders or licence endorsements. However, the fact that the main sentencing change was in the opposite direction to that anticipated is surprising, especially as it occurred in relation to seven of the twelve types of offences for which it had been employed in the 'before' period and did not seem to be a consequence of changes in the mix of cases coming before the courts for sentence. As noted in Chapter 1 a similar change was reported by Mortimer and Mair (1996) from the hypothetical sentencing exercise conducted shortly after the Green Paper was published.

Table 5.1:   Teesside – sentencing for principal offence[18]

| | Magistrates' courts | | Crown Court | |
| | Before | After | Before | After |
	%	%	%	%
Discharge	19	21	-	1
Fine	39	41	1	-
Community sentences	26	21	35	34
Prison	14	13	63	63
Other	2	4	-	2
All cases (N)	2,394	2,911	392	522

There were also significant changes *within* the community penalty sentencing band at magistrates' courts: the proportion of offenders receiving community service (CS) orders fell by nearly half; and combination orders and probation orders with additional requirements, which had accounted for one-third of all community penalties imposed in the 'before' period, rose to half of such orders in the 'after' period (Table 5.2). At the Crown Court, straight probation and CS, which together had accounted for three-quarters of community penalties passed, fell to less than 60 per cent, being offset by a rise in probation with requirements and a smaller (non-significant) rise in combination orders.

Table 5.2:   Teesside – use of community sentences

| | Magistrates' courts | | Crown Court | |
| | Before | After | Before | After |
	%	%	%	%
Probation	35	33	28	17
Community service	32	17	46	40
Probation with requirements	18	28	9	22
Combination orders	15	22	17	22
All cases (N)	632	596	138	176

18   Columns in some Tables may not sum to 100 per cent because of rounding.

The number of offenders sentenced in the 'after' period in Shropshire was nearly one-third higher at both court levels than the number in the 'before' period (Table 5.3). At the magistrates' court level, there was a significant increase in the use of discharges and a similar sized decrease in the use of fines. There was also an increase in the use of 'other' penalties but the overall use of community penalties and prison were unaltered. At the Crown Court, however, there was a significant increase in the proportion receiving community sentences and a decrease in the proportion being imprisoned. While these results relate to fairly small numbers, the differences are significant.

Table 5.3: Shropshire – sentencing for principal offence

| | Magistrates' courts | | Crown Court | |
| | Before | After | Before | After |
	%	%	%	%
Discharge	21	25	<1	1
Fine	45.5	41	3	7
Community sentences	22	22	22	31
Prison	8.5	8	74.5	58
Other	2	5	0	2
All cases (N)	1,022	1,357	165	215

Sentencing changes *within* the community sentence band at Shropshire's magistrates' courts followed a similar pattern to that in Teesside. In other words, the proportion receiving probation and CS orders fell and the proportion receiving probation orders with additional requirements and combination orders rose (see Table 5.4). However, only the changes in the use of CS and probation orders with requirements reached statistical significance.

Table 5.4: Shropshire – use of community sentences

| | Magistrates' courts | | Crown Court | |
| | Before | After | Before | After |
	%	%	%	%
Probation	31	24	28	19
Community service	40	29	53	52
Probation with requirements	12	25.5	3	25
Combination orders	17	21	17	3
All cases (N)	228	294	36	67

At Shrewsbury Crown Court, within the community penalty band, the proportion of cases receiving probation orders with additional requirements rose from 3 per cent to 25 per cent; and the proportion sentenced to combination orders dropped from 17 per cent to 3 per cent. Both changes were statistically significant, although the numbers involved were small.

Were these changes unique to the project areas?

As a proportion of all sentences across England and Wales, the use of community penalties for the 'before' and 'after' periods remained constant, at 8 per cent for magistrates' courts and 27 per cent for the Crown Court[19]. The proportion of magistrates' court cases being sentenced to community penalties is lower than that in each of the project areas, because it includes the very large number of cases where offenders pleaded guilty by post. In these cases, the principal offence (mainly minor motoring offences such as speeding) is almost invariably dealt with by means of a fine.

As Table 5.5 shows, within the community penalty range the national breakdown is very similar to that in the project areas (see Tables 5.2 and 5.4 above) in the 'before' period, but the increased use of probation orders with requirements and decreased use of CS in the 'after' period are barely discernible.

Table 5.5: England and Wales – use of community sentences

	Magistrates' courts		Crown Court	
	Before	After	Before	After
	%	%	%	%
Probation	35	36	33	33
Community service	38	36	46	44
Probation with requirements	11	11	4	5
Combination orders	15	16	17	17
All cases (N)	44,324	48,040	9,866	10,916

How were sentencing changes related to the offences for which offenders were convicted?

In order to understand what drove the sentencing changes in each area, it is important to know how they related to the types of cases coming before sentencers in the two areas. First, therefore, we considered whether the offence breakdown changed. Second, the rise in the use of probation orders with additional requirements, in both areas and at both court levels, is considered.

19   These figures and those shown in Table 5.5 were generated specially for this study by RDS colleagues with responsiblity for sentencing statistics.

There were three statistically significant changes in the types of offence sentenced at the magistrates' courts in Teesside:

* the number and proportion sentenced for burglary fell from 7 per cent (N=160) to 3 per cent (N=85);

* the number and proportion for summary motoring offences fell – from 25 per cent (N=597) to 20 per cent (589); and

* the number and proportion of offenders sentenced for non-motoring summary offences increased significantly, from 22 per cent (N=521)) to 31 per cent (N=914).

Table 5.6: Teesside – offences for sentence

	Magistrates' courts		Crown Court	
	Before	After	Before	After
	%	%	%	%
Violence	3	3	14.5	15
Sex	1	2	3	2.5
Burglary	7	3	28	24
Robbery	-	-	3	5
Theft (indictable)	33	32	18	16.5
Fraud and forgery	3	4	2	3
Criminal damage	<1	<1	2	1
Drugs	3	2	9	11
Other indictable (exc motoring)	2	2	11	10
Indictable motoring	<1	-	2	3
Summary (exc motoring)*	22	31	6	4
Summary motoring*	25	20	1	2
Missing	2	<1	<1	2
All cases (N)	2,394	2,911	392	522

*   The principal offence may be a summary one at the Crown Court if indictable charges are withdrawn or result in an acquittal.

As the *number* of burglars fell while the *proportion* sentenced to a probation order with requirements rose slightly (from 12% to 13%), this involved eight fewer people receiving such orders in the 'after' period (see Table 5.7).

The use of probation orders with requirements for summary non-motoring offences also only rose by one percentage point, from just under 4 per cent to nearly 5 per cent. Because there was such a large increase in the number of such cases this involved a further 22 orders.

The largest proportionate change in sentencing related to summary motoring offences, where the proportion receiving a probation order with requirements rose from 2 per cent to 6 per cent – an increase of 24 people. At the same time the use of CS fell from 9 per cent to 4 per cent, and straight probation also dropped by one percentage point, to 4 per cent.

In other words, these results show that the proportionate use of probation orders with additional requirements increased slightly for burglary, but because there were fewer such cases sentenced this did not add to the overall increase in such orders. There was also a small proportionate increase in the use of probation orders with requirements for summary non-motoring cases. Because of the large increase in such cases this did contribute to the overall rise in such orders. However, the most obvious change in sentencing behaviour was the increased use of probation orders with requirements for summary motoring cases.

Most of the increase in probation orders with requirements not explained by these offences was due to its use for ten 'other indictable' (mainly public order) offences in the 'after' period compared with one case in the 'before' period. Such cases comprised 2 per cent of the caseload in both study periods.

Table 5.7: Teesside – number of offenders sentenced to probation orders with additional requirements within each offence group*

| | Magistrates' courts | | | | Crown Court | | | |
| | Before | | After | | Before | | After | |
	n	%	n	%	n	%	n	%
Violence	12	(15)	10	(12)	1	(2)	4	(5)
Sex	-		1	(2)	-		-	
Burglary	19	(12)	11	(13)	3	(3)	10	(8)
Robbery	-		-		-		-	
Theft (indictable)	41	(5)	45	(5)	5	(7)	10	(11)
Fraud and forgery	7	(10)	6	(6)	1	(11)		-
Criminal damage	-		4	(33)	-		1	(20)
Drugs	1	(2)	1	(1.5)	-		4	(7)
Other indictable (exc motoring)	1	(2.5)	10	(19)	2	(5)	3	(6)
Indictable motoring	-		-		-		-	
Summary (exc motoring)	20	(4)	42	(5)	-		2	(9)
Summary motoring	13	(2)	37	(6)	-		4	(36)
Missing	1	(2.5)	1	(8)	-		-	
All cases (N)	115		168		12		38	

* Because of the small N, raw numbers are presented with percentages in parentheses.

As Table 5.6 shows, there were no significant changes in the types of offender being sentenced in the 'before' and 'after' periods at the Crown Court in Teesside. Table 5.7 shows that the increased use of probation with requirements there occurred across a wide range of offences, including more serious ones such as burglary, violence and drugs. Thus, the increased use of probation orders with additional requirements is not simply due to changes in the types of case coming to the Crown Court, but reflects a change in sentencing behaviour.

Overall, there is no evidence that the demonstration project in Teesside increased sentencers' confidence in community penalties compared with other sentencing options. When considered in the light of the views sentencers expressed about the purpose of different community sentences (see Chapter 3) it seems likely that the increased use of probation orders with requirements reflects an increased belief that this particular form of community penalty can prevent reoffending. At the Crown Court, this seems to have affected the sentencing of a broad range of offences, including violence and burglary. However, magistrates seemed most willing to alter their sentencing behaviour in relation to drunken drivers, who made up two-thirds of the summary motoring category, and those convicted of driving while disqualified, who accounted for most of the other cases.

Given that sentencers consider the main purpose of CS to be providing reparation, the reduction in the use of this sentence, may indicate that they believe this to be a less important objective than preventing reoffending.

At the Crown Court in Shropshire the only significant change in offence breakdown was the rise in sex offences and in the cases where we were unable to ascertain the type of offence. It is clear from Table 5.9, however, that these changes did not explain the increased use of probation orders with additional requirements that, as at Teesside Crown Court centre, occurred across a wide range of offences.

Table 5.8: Shropshire – offences for sentence

	Magistrates' courts		Crown Court	
	Before	After	Before	After
	%	%	%	%
Violence	5	4	25.5	18
Sex	<1	<1	2	6.5
Burglary	4	2	18	18
Robbery	<1	0	7	5
Theft (indictable)	21	16	13	8
Fraud and forgery	3	2	1	4
Criminal damage	3	5	4	3
Drugs	3	4	6	11
Other indictable (exc motoring)	2	3	21	16
Indictable motoring	1	1	0	1
Summary (exc motoring)	22	32	1	2
Summary motoring	34	30	0	4
Missing	1	0	2	6
All cases (N)	1,022	1,357	165	215

At the magistrates' courts in Shropshire by far the largest change in offence type was that the proportion of non-motoring summary offences rose from 22 per cent before CSDP to 32 per cent in the 'after' period, reflecting the fact that the number of such cases nearly doubled (225 to 440). There were two other significant changes in the types of case in that:

- the proportion accounted for by summary motoring cases fell from 34 per cent to 30 per cent, although the number of such cases increased from 349 to 411; and

- indictable thefts fell significantly from 21 per cent to 16 per cent, while the numbers remained relatively steady (219 to 222).

Table 5.9: *Shropshire – number of offenders sentenced to probation orders with additional requirements within each offence group**

| | Magistrates' courts | | | | Crown Court | | | |
| | Before | | After | | Before | | After | |
	n	%	n	%	n	%	n	%
Violence	4	(8)	7	(13)	1	(2)	4	(10.5)
Sex		-	1	(33)		-	2	(14)
Burglary	7	(18)	3	(11)		-	3	(8)
Robbery	-	-	-	-				
Theft (indictable)	4	(2)	5	(2)		-		-
Fraud and forgery	1	(3)	3	(14)		-		-
Criminal damage	2	(6.5)	3	(4)			2	(33)
Drugs		-	1	(2)		-		-
Other indictable (exc motoring)	2	(8)	2	(4)		-	3	(9)
Indictable motoring	1	(14)	4	(50)		-		-
Summary (exc motoring)	2	(1)	14	(3)		-	1	(20)
Summary motoring	4	(1)	32	(8)		-	1	(25)
Missing	1	(9)		-		-	1	(8)
All cases (N)	28		75		1		17	

*   Because of the small N, raw numbers are presented with percentages in parentheses

The proportion of those convicted of indictable theft who received a probation order with additional requirements in the 'before' period compared with the 'after' period remained steady at around 2 per cent. The increase in the proportion of summary non-motoring offences sentenced in this way rose from 1 per cent to 3 per cent and thus contributed to the overall rise in the use of this sentence. However, as in Teesside, most of the change was explained by the rise in the proportion of summary motoring offenders being sentenced to probation with requirements (1% to 8%). It is, of course, important to recognise that the proportion of violence, fraud and forgery and indictable motoring offences being sentenced in this way also rose.

The Shropshire Crown Court results generally indicate a greater willingness to use community penalties in place of custody, although the change was most marked in relation to probation orders with requirements. As in Teesside, however, the main change in magistrates' use of such orders related to drink-driving and driving while disqualified, which together accounted for well over 90 per cent of summary motoring cases.

How far did sentencing decisions reflect pre-sentence report proposals?

The main sentencing change in both areas was that the proportion of offenders being dealt with by means of a probation order with additional requirements increased. As the increase mainly related to summary motoring, it is important to know what caused this change. Was it because the courts acted without probation advice or because there was a greater degree of agreement between what PSRs proposed and the sentences courts imposed? It would seem that there is support for both explanations in Teesside where on one hand a PSR was available in *fewer* cases where a probation order with requirements was imposed in the 'after' period at the magistrates' courts (down from 100% to 91%) and at the Crown Court (down 83% to 71%). On the other hand, in those cases where a PSR was available, the proportion of such sentences that matched the proposal increased from 78 per cent to 90 per cent.

In Shropshire, a PSR was available in *all* the cases in which a probation order with requirements was imposed in the 'before' period and in all but one (Crown Court) case in the 'after' period. However, the proportion of probation orders with additional requirements that had been suggested in PSRs *fell* from 65 per cent in the 'before' period to 54 per cent in the 'after' period, showing that the increased use of such orders as not driven by the Probation Service.

To what extent did pre-sentence report sentencing proposals reflect sentencers' views (shown on adjournment forms) about offence seriousness?

In order to investigate how far adjournment forms (Appendix B) affected PSR sentencing proposals and were related to actual sentencing, 287 forms were provided by the Teesside Service in relation to the 'after' period. In 124 (43%) of these the Bench considered seriousness to be substantial; 139 (48%) moderate, and 18 (6%) cases seriousness was considered low[20]. In six cases no view of seriousness was recorded. Where possible, these forms were then matched with PSR proposals and sentencing data. This was only achieved in 147 (51%) cases because identifying information was often missing from the forms (see Table 5.10)[21].

---

20   It is not clear how closely these three groupings were intended to match the Criminal Justice Act 1991 definitions of seriousness, under which a community sentence was viewed as suitable for offences which were 'serious enough' but not 'so serious' that no other penalty but custody could be justified.

21   The number of cases in which matches could not be made was high. However, this is unlikely to have biased the results as the proportions of matched and unmatched cases in which the court viewed the offence seriousness as substantial, moderate or low are broadly similar.

Table 5.10: Indications of seriousness

	Substantial (%)	Moderate (%)	Low (%)
Matched to sentenced cases (N=147)	46	48	6
Unmatched (N=138)	42	51	7
All (N=281)	44	49	6

Table 5.11 shows the view of seriousness expressed by the commissioning Bench with the resulting PSR proposal. The sentence column in this table shows the sentences used within each of the three seriousness levels. Of course the numbers are very small, but the results indicate that magistrates may see combination orders and custody as suitable sentences for offences of substantial seriousness, whereas probation officers are proposing probation orders with additional requirements.

Table 5.11: Indications of seriousness – number of proposals and sentences

	Substantial		Moderate		Low	
	proposal	sentence	proposal	sentence	proposal	sentence
Probation	12	9	24	27	3	2
CS	11	9	6	5	-	-
Probation with requirements	20	12	19	15	2	2
Combination order	12	22	2	7	-	2
Custody	0	11	0	5	-	-
Other	11	3	18	10	3	2
All (N=147)	66	66	69	69	8	8

Table 5.12 shows how often each individual proposal was followed. Perhaps the most interesting feature of this table is the column totals, which suggest that the likelihood of the court following a sentence proposal decreases as seriousness increases. It is also worth noting that in 29 of the 31 cases where the court considered seriousness to be substantial and did not follow a sentencing proposal, the actual sentence was more severe than the one proposed. This was true of 22 of the 27 moderate or low seriousness cases where the sentencing proposal was not followed.

Table 5.12: Teesside proposals and sentences according to indications of seriousness

	Substantial		Moderate		Low	
	proposal	sentence	proposal	sentence	proposal	sentence
Probation	12	7	24	20	3	2
CS	11	7	6	4	-	-
Probation with requirements	20	9	19	11	2	1
Combination order	12	10	2	1	-	-
Other	11	2	18	9	3	2
All (N=147)	66	35	69	45	8	5

Key findings

The comparison of sentencing practice before and after the demonstration projects began revealed that:

- sentencing changes in both areas did not seem to be a reflection of national sentencing patterns; nor were they simply a consequence of changes in the types of case being sentenced;

- the overall proportion of offenders receiving community penalties was unchanged at Teesside Crown Court and in the magistrates' courts in Shropshire;

- there was a decline in the use of community penalties in the Teesside magistrates' courts which could not be explained in terms of changes in the types of case for sentence;

- at the Crown Court in Shropshire, the proportions fined and awarded community sentences rose and the proportion being imprisoned fell; these results relate to fairly small numbers, but the differences are significant;

- the use of probation orders with additional requirements increased at the Crown Court and magistrates' courts in both areas, perhaps reflecting a greater belief in this sentence's power to prevent reoffending; in most cases the rise was associated with a decreased use of CS, the main aim of which is perceived to be reparation;

- the increased use of probation orders with additional requirements occurred across a wide range of offences at both Crown Court centres; however, at the magistrates' courts it was most marked in relation to offenders convicted of summary motoring offences;

- to some extent the increased use of probation orders with additional requirements at the magistrates' court level seems to have been brought about by sentencers using such disposals without adjourning for PSRs. However, when PSRs were available the proportion of such sentences that matched proposals increased in Teesside and decreased in Shropshire.

6 Conclusions

This research set out to address ten questions:

- did the Probation Service improve the range of community service (CS) or probation programmes?

- did the Probation Service improve the information available to sentencers about CS or probation programmes?

- did sentencers seek and/or receive more feedback on success rates?

- did sentencers give probation officers clearer guidance when requesting pre-sentence reports (PSRs)?

- did sentencers express more confidence in community sentences?

- did sentencers make clearer sentencing pronouncements?

- did the use of community sentences increase during the demonstration period?

- was there an improvement in enforcement action?

- did the sentencers and probation staff involved in the projects think they had been a success and what other changes would they like to see?

- did newspaper, TV or radio reporting of local sentencing decisions and the use of community sentences alter?

The answers the research has provided are considered in this chapter.

No new programmes were set up in Shropshire during the course of the demonstration projects. Instead the Local Steering Group decided that they should focus on ensuring that sentencers and the public had a much clearer idea of what actually happened to someone serving a community sentence. Teesside Probation Service used the project to push forward several initiatives, such as reviewing and revising the content of their probation programmes. They also ensured that sentencers were provided with more detailed information about the content of community penalties. As a result of these changes sentencers described themselves as much more satisfied with the information they received about the number of places on CS and probation programmes and when an offender would start a specified activity.

Magistrates in both areas felt that they could more closely tailor sentences to an individual offender's needs as a consequence of the demonstration projects. In fact, many thought that there had been more changes to the range of probation programmes and types of CS available that had actually occurred. This reflects the fact that they were much better informed about what was available because of the efforts the two Probation Services had put into disseminating this information. The most striking change was the increase in the proportion of magistrates in each area that believed probation orders with additional requirements had the capacity to prevent reoffending.

A small number of sentencers felt that legislation was needed to combine sentences in new ways. The most popular combination was a short custodial sentence followed by some form of community penalty. It is open to question how useful such a change would be given that American research suggests that such sentences have lower success rates than others (Langan, 1994).

Judges and magistrates in both areas were given the opportunity to be more specific about what they would like PSRs to cover, by completing a checklist of offenders' needs and an adjournment form that indicated how seriously they viewed an offence. In interview most sentencers thought the new forms were very useful and observation of court hearings in both areas suggests that towards the end of the year-long demonstration period, magistrates were using them regularly.

Techniques used to promote compliance were largely unaffected by the projects; however, sentencers in the 'after' period felt significantly better informed about supervision arrangements for all types of community order than in the 'before' period. In Shropshire magistrates' satisfaction with the supervision and enforcement of all community penalties improved during the demonstration project, perhaps reflecting the greater speed with which breaches were brought to court. In Teesside the change was only significant in the case of probation orders with requirements and combination orders. Crown Court sentencers' satisfaction with enforcement declined. They were partly concerned about the Probation Service being too slow to take breach action, but their comments also concerned aspects of the process that were beyond the control of the Probation Service.

Shropshire and Teesside Probation Services were willing to provide information to sentencers on completion and breach, either on an individual basis or aggregated across cases. Both had tried various means to make this information easily accessible. The apparently contradictory finding that the majority of sentencers wanted feedback in individual cases, but that most never asked for any, may reflect the fact that they do not want this information on every individual they sentence, but on the few where they are particularly concerned about an offender's progress. Sentencers would welcome aggregated data on all offenders, however, in order to better judge the value of individual programmes and types of order.

Four out of five magistrates in both areas were 'always' or 'frequently' influenced in their choice of sentence by PSRs in the 'before' period and most thought that PSR proposals were generally appropriate. Probably for this reason there was no improvement on either of these dimensions as a result of the demonstration projects.

Judges were less inclined to call for a PSR or to say that it influenced their decision-making, but this was because they saw imposing a community sentence as taking a risk – believing that most of the cases they dealt with were firmly within the custody band.

Both groups of sentencers were equivocal on whether more proposals for custody in PSRs would increase their confidence in the Probation Service in general.

One of the ways in which the demonstration projects were expected to enhance the credibility of community sentences was by making sentencing pronouncements clearer so that offenders were told why they were being sentenced in particular ways and what would happen should they fail to comply. However, over half (13) of the probation staff who attended court regularly in Shropshire said this rarely or never happened, as did slightly less than half (11) of those in Teesside. Our own smallscale observation in a magistrates' court in each area confirmed that sentencing pronouncements were rare.

At Shrewsbury Crown Court there was an increase in the proportion of offenders being fined and receiving a community sentence and a decrease in the proportion being imprisoned, but the numbers involved were small. There was no other evidence that the demonstration projects encouraged the greater use of community penalties as an alternative to custody. Indeed, the overall use of community penalties in magistrates' courts in Teesside actually declined during the demonstration project. The reasons for this are not obvious.

The only sentencing change common to both areas and both court levels was that the proportion of cases receiving probation orders with additional requirements increased.

It seems likely that this reflects an increased belief that this particular form of community penalty can prevent reoffending. At the Crown Court this seems to have affected the use of such sentences for a broad range of offences, including violence and burglary. However, magistrates seemed most willing to alter their sentencing behaviour in relation to drunken drivers and those convicted of driving while disqualified, who make up most of the summary motoring category, although the sentencing of other offences was also affected.

To some extent the increased use of probation orders with additional requirements in magistrates' courts seems to have been brought about by sentencers using such disposals without adjourning for PSRs. When PSRs were available the proportion of such sentences that matched proposals increased in Teesside and decreased in Shropshire.

Sentencers considered the main purpose of CS to be for reparation. The fact that they used this sentence less often once the demonstration project began may indicate that they believe it to be a less important objective than preventing reoffending.

A majority of sentencers and probation staff thought the demonstration projects had been useful. For sentencers, it provided an opportunity to be more directive about what they wanted PSRs to focus on and the content of individual sentences. For probation staff, the positive effects were an increased use of probation programmes, better relationships with sentencers and a better understanding of what sentencers wanted PSRs to concentrate on. However, some were concerned that sentencing had become less appropriate, with sentencers imposing probation orders with requirements on offenders who were not capable of meeting the demands such orders imposed. This highlights the need to ensure that decisions about effectiveness are tempered by considerations of proportionality. However, the lack of a clear tariff for community sentences makes this difficult to achieve, as various commentators, including Rex (1998), have noted.

As the new Crime Reduction Programme project on community service gets off the ground and the joint Home Office, ACOP, HMI Probation initiative on effective practice and supervision goes forward, it will be important to ensure that sentencers are made more fully aware of what is known to be effective in reducing reoffending so that effectiveness is not assumed to reside only in group work accessed through a statutory requirement to attend.

Newspaper reports of sentencing before and after the projects took place showed that while crime was frequently reported, only one-quarter of articles mentioned sentencing. Also, sentencing almost never hit the front page (3% of 273 articles, compared with 10% of crime reporting).

Interestingly, while sex, violence and theft were discussed in half of all newspaper reports on crime, motoring was the next most common topic. In Teesside this proportion rose from 7 per cent in the 'before' period to 13 per cent in the 'after' period. It is not possible to say whether this reporting led to the change in sentencing of summary motoring cases or was a product of it.

Overall, the demonstration projects showed that better communication improved relations between the Probation Service and sentencers and that this was something both sides welcomed. While this is undoubtedly an important first step in promoting the greater use of community sentences, the results of this study suggest that this does not, by itself, lead to a significant increase in the use of community penalties and the question of whether new legislation is required must be revisited.

References

Charles, N., Whittaker, C., and Ball, C. (1997) *Sentencing without a pre-sentence report*. Research Findings No. 47. London: Home Office.

Ellis, T., Hedderman, C. and Mortimer, E. (1996) *Enforcing community sentences*. Home Office Research Study No. 158. London: Home Office.

Flood-Page, C. and Mackie, A. (1998) *Sentencing Practice: an examination of decisions in magistrates' courts and the Crown Court in the mid-1990s*. Home Office Research Study No. 180. London: Home Office.

Hansen, A. (1999) *Local Media Coverage of Crime and Sentencing*. Unpublished report to the Home Office.

Hedderman, C. and Moxon, D. (1992) *Magistrates' Court or Crown Court? Mode of trial decisions and sentencing*. Home Office Research Study No. 125. London: HMSO.

Home Affairs Committee (1998) *Alternatives to prison sentences*. Volume 1 Report and Proceedings of the Committee. London: Stationery Office.

Home Office (1995a) *National Standards for the Supervision of Offenders in the Community*. London: HMSO.

Home Office (1995b) *Strengthening Punishment in the Community*. London: HMSO. Command Paper 2780.

Home Office (1997a) *Criminal Statistics, 1996*. London: Home Office.

Home Office (1997b) *Probation Statistics, 1996*. London: Home Office.

Hough, M. and Roberts, J (1998) *Attitudes to punishment: findings from the 1996 British Crime Survey*. Research Findings No 64. London: Home Office.

Kish, L. (1965) *Survey Sampling*. New York: John Wiley.

Klein-Saffran, J. (1992) 'The Development of Intermediate Punishments at the Federal Level', in Byrne, J. M., Lurigio, A. J. and Petersilia, J. (Eds) *Smart Sentencing: The Emergence of Intermediate Sanctions.* Newbury Park: Sage.

Langan, P. A. (1994) 'Between Prison and Probation: Intermediate Sanctions', *Science,* Volume 264, pp 791-793.

May, C. (1995) *Measuring the satisfaction of the Courts with the Probation Service.* Home Office Research Study No. 144. London: Home Office.

Mortimer, E. and Mair, G (1996) *Integrating community sentences: the results from the green paper sentencing exercises.* Unpublished report to the Home Office.

ONS (1997) *Regional Trends No 32.* London: Office of National Statistics.

Rex, S. (1998) 'Applying desert principles to community sentences: lessons from two Criminal Justice Acts', *Criminal Law Review,* 1998.

Appendix A

TEESSIDE MAGISTRATES' COURT
Community Sentence Demonstration Project

CHECKLIST

PLEASE
INVESTIGATE

1. Q.	Does the defendant have any disabilities which would prevent him from completing a community order?			
A.		Yes ☐	No ☐	

2a) Q.	Domestic situation/Lifestyle			
A		Yes ☐	No ☐	
2b) Q.	Educational background/Career opportunities			
A		Yes ☐	No ☐	
2c) Q.	Achievments/Failures			
A.		Yes ☐	No ☐	

3. Q. Did motivation for the offence include any of the following

a) Q.	Drug/Alcohol addiction			
A.		Yes ☐	No ☐	
b) Q.	Financial circumstances/unemployment			
A.		Yes ☐	No ☐	
c) Q.	Peer Pressure			
A.		Yes ☐	No ☐	
d) Q.	Mental health problems			
A.		Yes ☐	No ☐	
e) Q.	Stress			
A.		Yes ☐	No ☐	
f) Q.	Anger/Aggression/Domestic violence			
A.		Yes ☐	No ☐	
g) Q.	Sexual misconduct			
A.		Yes ☐	No ☐	

4. Q.	Response to previous community penalties			
A.		Yes ☐	No ☐	
5. Q.	Has the defendant made any voluntary reparation			
A.		Yes ☐	No ☐	
6. Q.	Has the defendant undergone any voluntary treatment for problems, eg drug addiction			
A.		Yes ☐	No ☐	
7. Q.	(Other)			
A.		Yes ☐	No ☐	

TO BE HANDED TO PROBATION IN COURT

Appendix B

TEESSIDE MAGISTRATES' COURT
Community Sentence Demonstration Project

ADJOURNMENT FOR PRE-SENTENCE REPORT

Date:
Name of defendant:
Charges:
Date of adjourned hearing:
Solicitor:

AT THIS STAGE in the proceedings, the following Preliminary Indications apply:

Seriousness:	Substantial
(restriction of liberty required)	Moderate
	Low
Purpose of Sentence	Reparation
	Restriction of Liberty
	Prevention of reoffending
Probation support to	☐ Accommodation
include advice on	☐ Making Headway
	☐ Finances
	☐ Other: please specify

Probation   Additional requirements (eg courses)

☐ Thinking straight
☐ Victim awareness   ☐ Handling conflict
☐ Alcohol awareness   ☐ Responsible drivers
☐ Citizenship   ☐ Drug awareness
☐ Job seekers guidance
☐ Residence in Hostel

Community Service   Specific work to be considered – list 3 in order of priority

1)
2)
3)

New Scheme to Consider:

Proposed time spent	☐ National Standard	☐ Excess of National
undertaking order	☐ Minimum	Standard Minimum

TO BE HANDED TO PROBATION IN COURT

Appendix C

SHROPSHIRE
Community Sentence Demonstration Project

ADJOURNMENT FOR PRE-SENTENCE REPORT

PRONOUNCEMENT

We think that this case is too serious for us to deal with today without a report. We are going to adjourn the case for three weeks for the Probation Service to prepare that report. The purpose of the report is to help the court reach a final decision about just how serious this offence is and then to go on to decide what happens to you (how you should be dealt with).

In three weeks' time, it will be up to the magistrate sitting that day to decide what to do; we can make you no promises today and you must understand that for this offence (these offences) you could be sent to prison (YOI) or given a community sentence, that is a probation order, a community service order, or a combination of both.

We want the Probation Service to:

• see what can be done to stop you doing this kind of thing again;

• consider whether prison or a community sentence will best match what you have done;

• see what can be done to make you pay back the community for what you have done.

Before you leave court, you must see the duty probation officer who will explain what arrangements will be made to prepare the report.

Unconditional/conditional bail/custody

Appendix D

COMMUNITY SENTENCE PRONOUNCEMENT

GENERAL OPENING

We have considered the facts of this case and have read the pre-sentence report. We think that this offence (these offences) is (are) serious enough to deserve a community sentence, because:

Outline reasons for 'serious enough' e.g.

- facts/number of particular offence(s);
- group action;
- committed at night;
- previous convictions;
- (the offences taken into consideration, etc)

We have taken into account:

- the fact that you pleaded guilty;
- (other mitigating factors)

PROBATION ORDER

We propose making a probation order for (one) year. That means that for the next year you would be under the supervision of a probation officer. You must keep out of trouble, you must make visits to the probation officer and receive visits at home if required; you must keep appointments with your probation officer. If you change your address you must tell your probation officer.

We are also going to include some extra conditions in the order. You must attend the:

- Motoring Offenders Education Project;
- Alcohol Education Project;
- Anger Management course.

You must live at a bail hostel or wherever the probation officer directs.

You must receive medical/psychiatric treatment is advised.

This/these conditions is/are imposed because we think it/they is/are necessary to try and stop you re-offending.

If you fail to comply with these conditions, you will be brought back to court and the order may be revoked (cancelled). In that case we start all over again and you would be re-sentenced for these offences.

Do you understand?

Do you agree to a probation order?

COMMUNITY SERVICE ORDER

We propose making a community service order for (100) hours. That means that you will be required to carry out (100) hours of unpaid work in your own time for the benefit of the community. You will be directed by the Probation Service; you must report as required and work satisfactorily.

If you fail to report, or to work satisfactorily, you will be brought back to court and the order may be revoked (cancelled). In that case we start all over again and you would be re-sentenced for these offences.

Do you understand?

Do you agree to a community service order?

COMBINATION ORDER

We propose making a combination order. This has two parts, probation and community service.

The first part means that for the next (year) you would be under the supervision of a probation officer. (Continue as probation order requirements above.)

The second part means that for (maximum 100 hours) you will be required to carry out unpaid work in your own time for the benefit of the community. (Continue as community service requirements above.)

If you fail to comply with the conditions of probation or community service, or both of them, you will be brought back to court and the order may be revoked (cancelled). In that case we start all over again and you would be re-sentenced for these offences.

Do you understand?

Do you agree to a combination order?

Publications

List of research publications

The most recent research reports published are listed below. A **full** list of publications is available on request from the Research, Development and Statistics Directorate, Information and Publications Group.

Home Office Research Studies (HORS)

184. **Remand decisions and offending on bail: evaluation of the Bail Process Project.** Patricia M Morgan and Paul F Henderson. 1998.

185. **Entry into the criminal justice system: a survey of police arrests and their outcomes.** Coretta Phillips and David Brown with the assistance of Zoë James and Paul Goodrich. 1998

186. **The restricted hospital order: from court to the community.** Robert Street. 1998

187. **Reducing Offending: An assessment of research evidence on ways of dealing with offending behaviour.** Edited by Peter Goldblatt and Chris Lewis. 1998.

188. **Lay visiting to police stations.** Mollie Weatheritt and Carole Vieira. 1998

189. **Mandatory drug testing in prisons: The relationship between MDT and the level and nature of drug misuse.** Kimmett Edgar and Ian O'Donnell. 1998

190. **Trespass and protest: policing under the Criminal Justice and Public Order Act 1994.** Tom Bucke and Zoë James. 1998.

191. **Domestic Violence: Findings from a new British Crime Survey self-completion questionnaire.** Catriona Mirrlees-Black. 1999.

192. **Explaining reconviction following a community sentence: the role of social factors.** Chris May. 1999.

Research Findings

60. **Policing and the public: findings from the 1996 British Crime Survey.** Catriona Mirrlees-Black and Tracy Budd. 1997.

61. **Changing offenders' attitudes and behaviour: what works?** Julie Vennard, Carol Hedderman and Darren Sugg. 1997.

62. **Suspects in police custody and the revised PACE codes of practice.** Tom Bucke and David Brown. 1997.

63. **Neighbourhood watch co-ordinators.** Elizabeth Turner and Banos Alexandrou. 1997.

64. **Attitudes to punishment: findings from the 1996 British Crime Survey.** Michael Hough and Julian Roberts. 1998.

65. **The effects of video violence on young offenders.** Kevin Browne and Amanda Pennell. 1998.

66. **Electronic monitoring of curfew orders: the second year of the trials.** Ed Mortimer and Chris May. 1998.

67. **Public perceptions of drug-related crime in 1997.** Nigel Charles. 1998.

68. **Witness care in magistrates' courts and the youth court.** Joyce Plotnikoff and Richard Woolfson. 1998.

69. **Handling stolen goods and theft: a market reduction approach.** Mike Sutton. 1998.

70. **Drug testing arrestees.** Trevor Bennett. 1998.

71. **Prevention of plastic card fraud.** Michael Levi and Jim Handley. 1998.

72. **Offending on bail and police use of conditional bail.** David Brown. 1998.

73. **Voluntary after-care.** Mike Maguire, Peter Raynor, Maurice Vanstone and Jocelyn Kynch. 1998.

74. **Fast-tracking of persistent young offenders.** John Graham. 1998.

75. **Mandatory drug testing in prisons – an evaluation.** Kimmett Edgar and Ian O'Donnell. 1998.

76. **The prison population in 1997: a statistical review.** Philip White. 1998.

77. **Rural areas and crime: findings from the British Crime Survey.** Catriona Mirrlees-Black. 1998.

78. **A review of classification systems for sex offenders.** Dawn Fisher and George Mair. 1998.

79. **An evaluation of the prison sex offender treatment programme.** Anthony Beech et al. 1998.

80. **Age limits for babies in prison: some lessons from abroad.** Diane Caddle. 1998.

81. **Motor projects in England & Wales: an evaluation.** Darren Sugg. 1998

82. **HIV/Aids risk behaviour among adult male prisoners.** John Strange et al. 1998.

83. **Concern about crime: findings from the 1998 British Crime Survey.** Catriona Mirrlees-Black and Jonathan Allen. 1998.

84. **Transfers from prison to hospital – the operation of section 48 of the Mental Health Act 1983.** Ronnie Mackay and David Machin. 1998.

85. **Evolving crack cocaine careers.** Kevin Brain, Howard Parker and Tim Bottomley. 1998.

86. **Domestic Violence: Findings from the BCS self-completion questionnaire.** Catriona Mirrlees-Black and Carole Byron. 1999.

87. **Incentives and earned privileges for prisoners – an evaluation.** Alison Liebling, Grant Muir, Gerry Rose and Anthony Bottoms. 1999.

88. **World prison population list.** Roy Walmsley. 1999.

89. **Probation employment schemes in Inner London and Surrey – an evaluation.** Chris Samo, Michael Hough, Claire Nee and Victoria Herrington. 1999.

Occasional Papers

Evaluation of a Home Office initiative to help offenders into employment. Ken Roberts, Alana Barton, Julian Buchanan and Barry Goldson. 1997.

The impact of the national lottery on the horse-race betting levy. Simon Field and James Dunmore. 1997.

The cost of fires. A review of the information available. Donald Roy. 1997.

Monitoring and evaluation of WOLDS remand prison and comparisons with public-sector prisons, in particular HMP Woodhill. A Keith Bottomley, Adrian James, Emma Clare and Alison Liebling. 1997.

Evaluation of the 'One Stop Shop' and victim statement pilot projects. Carolyn Hoyle, Ed Cape, Rod Morgan and Andrew Sanders. 1998.

Step 3: an evaluation of the prison sex offender treatment programme. Anthony Beech, Dawn Fisher and Richard Beckett. 1998.

Requests for Publications

Home Office Research Studies, Research Findings and *Occasional Papers* can be requested from:

Research, Development and Statistics Directorate
Information and Publications Group
Room 201, Home Office
50 Queen Anne's Gate
London SW1H 9AT
Telephone: 0171-273 2084
Facsimile: 0171-222 0211
Internet: http://www.homeoffice.gov.uk/rds/index.htm
E-mail: rds.ho@gtnet.gov.uk